THEN CAME THE GLORY

BY

NONA FREEMAN

THEN CAME THE GLORY

NONA FREEMAN

Cover Design: Jo Elen Macon

All scriptures used in this text are taken from the King James Version of the Bible.

ISBN # 1-878366-08-4

First Printing 1994

To order contact: Nona's Book Sales
                        P.O. Box 0842
                        Minden, LA 71058-0842

Phone: (318) 377-9517 or (318) 377-6919

Printed in the United States of America by Faith Printing Co.

THANKS

Please accept my expression of gratitude to those who have generously given their time, welcome advice, and means to help with this project:

Brother Teklemariam Gehazagne, who worked tirelessly gathering information from far and near to complete the Amharic manuscript he gave me in February, 1993.

My Bug, whose priceless understanding and love has kept me going when going got tough.

Nell Perry, esteemed editor and friend whose tireless efforts and expertise shaped the finished book.

Jo Macon, whose talented painting and spiritual guidance always comes through.

Asrat Mengesha Arku, the Ethiopian Bible School student at Nairobi, Kenya who spent tedious hours writing by hand the translation from the original Amharic manuscript into English.

Tadesse Atsebeha, for information, concern, prayer and corrections.

Ethiopian Commentator Periodical, credit for excerpts and pertinent information.

Brother J.P. Hughes, RFS for Africa, who loaned me pictures.

Brother Cogo and Stockton Video Services for the loan of pictures.

Peggy Carter, who cleaned my house giving me more time to work on this lengthy project.

And most important of all, dear Jesus, my Friend who helped me through all the road blocks and computer traumas that hindered the work.

INTRODUCTION

Come with me to an ancient land whose record begins in the first chapter of Genesis. Their history unfolds with fierce warriors, capable of merciless cruelty and devout people whose yearning to worship plunged them into bizarre superstition.

Their long-reigning Emperor Haile Selassie captured the imagination of the Western world, most of whom did not realize he ruthlessly kept his country in the dark ages for his own self interest. A reporter who spent time there in 1937 told of nobles who displeased the Despot and he reduced them to the status of dogs, chained with collars who fawned at his feet for food. Yet the country stopped their clocks and calendars when Selassie went into exile during the second world war.

With a population that spans a tremendous cultural gap from nomads in the desert to well educated nobility in gracious homes, this mysterious land has survived everything from rapacious warlords to the rape of communism. A hunger for truth still grips its populace enhanced by an amazing capacity for loyalty. And God, in His infinite wisdom has chosen to show the world the true meaning of the word *revival* against a background of unbelievable suffering. Stripped of decency and barest necessities, the Ethiopians have found perfected agape love and the flow of exemplary unity that allows the King of Kings to move in ways unknown to most of us.

I do not expect you to understand or even believe all you read in these pages, but every miracle and inexplicable happening is authenticated. Let me remind you Jesus Christ recognizes integrity of heart and simple child-like faith. In our world *things*, and a desire for honor has replaced greater values and we suffer from dire poverty of spirit. May the example of the greatest recorded outpouring of God's Spirit in the history of the earth bring us to the promised move of

God through His Word that the Western world desperately needs.

If we shed our veneer of sophistication, discard our polished manipulations, strip off our masquerades of piety and explode our apathy and fear of being uncomfortable, it CAN happen on the rest of the globe!

Straw hut in a country village

The old dutchman

DEDICATION

I dedicate this book to the memory of an old Dutchman named Paulus who, directed by God,walked from Holland to Asfaw's house in Addis Ababa and declared: "God told me to come to Ethiopia and tell the people who He is and that He wants to live in their hearts in the power of the Holy Ghost, speaking with other tongues."

Handicapped by the language, he won no souls, though he made a lasting impression on all who saw him. He fasted forty days every year and foretold: "The name of Jesus will rise over Ethiopia, mightier than the sun."

After one fast he leaped out of his room and hung in the air one yard above the floor while he prophesied: "A mighty revival will sweep across Ethiopia and great miracles will be done in the name of Jesus. The Holy Ghost will be poured upon you, my friends."

Ayele Asfaw who heard that prophesy as a teenager, today pastors Gofa church with five thousand members.

Nona Freeman

The E.L.Freeman Conference Center in
Addis Ababa that seats ten thousand

TABLE OF CONTENTS

DEFINITION OF AMHARIC TERMS

Derg or PMAC: Provisional Military Administrative Council

EPRP: Ethiopian People Revolutionary Party

MESON: All Ethiopian Socialist Movement

EPRDF: Ethiopian Peoples Revolutionary Democratic Front

EPLF: Eritrean People Liberation Front

Ato: Title of Mister

Chat: A green leaf chewed by Moslems, Arabs, Somalis, Djiboutes,and Ethiopians which contains high quantities of nicotine--intolerable if addicted.

Malathine: A poisonous pesticide and insecticide

Holy water: The orthodox people name a spring having hot or cold water for an angel or a martyr and believe the water will heal the sick or deliver from devils. It may be a container of water prayed over and sprinkled on the patient.

Kale Hiwot: Word of Life

Mistirawian: Members of a secret Society

Pentes: A scornful slang term for the Pentecostals

CHAPTER ONE

BACKDROP OF HORROR

"Ethiopia first without blood shed!" Men inspired by dreams of democracy proclaimed the slogan loudly as they seized and caged in chains their cruel long-time Emperor, Haile Selasse, in 1974. His grand titles, King of Kings, Elected by God, Conqueror of the Lion of Judah, did not save his life, and the people rejoiced in waves of hope for a brighter future. With the Emperor's decree against the Pentecostals in 1971, they appropriately changed their name to Apostolics. Now, they reckoned the decree died with the Emperor and in jubilation the Apostolics anticipated freedom to worship and propagate the Gospel. Little did they realize the depths of anguish that lay ahead.

Even as the people dreamed of liberty to build a better land, the military hijacked the peoples' revolution and commandeered the government. Men trained only to shoot and kill formed the ruling Committee known as the Derg with Menguistu Hailemariam at the helm.

These fanatical communists launched the era called "Red Terror", vast enough in scope to be rightly labeled the African holocaust. They subjected the Ethiopian people to an appalling magnitude of horror, suffering, and bloodshed beyond comprehension by the Western world. they began with the murder of sixty senior officials, large numbers of students and religious leaders, and anyone else whom they disliked or who opposed them. Their wholesale slaughter obliterated entire villages and towns. In places they selected random innocent victims and ravaged whole areas in the countryside to frighten people into subjection. People who missed the bombs either starved to death or got rounded up like cattle and shipped to "villagization centers".

Some still cannot forget the dead bodies lying here and there on city sidewalks. Families who risked claiming the bodies of their loved ones had to pay a fee for the bullet that took their lives. many families did not know where to look for the bodies of missing members and the Derg forbade all of them to mourn, to share their grief, or to offer each other solace in the time-honored tradition of all faiths.

The "Red Terror" began in the middle of 1975 and continued until 1977. Sons killed their fathers, and brothers betrayed each other. The terror focused on young students and women in the provinces, streets and bars. The EPRP and the MESPM killed each other with automatic rifles. It became especially risky for the house to house fellowship. When the politicians met to plan the next attack, they placed an open Bible on a table for a blind. when the government perceived this tactic, they arrested and tortured everyone found in a meeting or fellowship. Mistaken for political opponents, many innocent people died.

When the Derg realized that churches and mosques attracted huge crowds of people seeking comfort and strength, they began a plan of infiltration into the leadership ranks of the Ethiopian Orthodox church. They found a man, known as Abba the Libanos, qualified in intrigue and murder to suit their purpose, member of a newly formed group in Addis Ababa, called Association of the Clergy. They rode roughshod over canonical objections and made him a Patriarch, called Archbishop Merkorious and transferred him to Gondar forcibly replacing a staunch opponent of "Red Terror" policies. The spurious Archbishop received high honors from his creators for the massive uprooting of Ethiopians and relocating them far from the community of their birth with such flagrant loss of life, the international community intervened to stop it.

The Archbishop made it his mission to turn Ethiopians into cogs and robots devoid of past and experience, a machine without the capacity for inquiry and critical thinking. Subservient robots willing to carry out repeated orders without questions. If all his shameful and tragic deeds could be recorded they would fill volumes of books. With the overthrow of communism, the Archbishop became an exile in another African country where he continues to deceive the unwise.

The Bible states explicitly, *Whoso sheddeth blood, by men shall his blood be shed.* Those who planned, pointed their fingers, and perpetrated this senseless bloodshed have since suffered severe agonies. They have been penalized and compelled to drink the bitter cup of death wherever they fled. Others died in horrible torment.

Thinking the Ethiopian military government had weakened, Somali began a war for possession of the Eastern region of Ethiopia, temporarily distracting the Military Government's opposition of most religions. The war provided relative rest for the believers, though the Derg continued the persecution until organized and armed opponents in Tigray and Eritrea attacked them. At this point the Derg sought cooperation from the nationalists, revolutionaries, and religious leaders. With the serious challenge from the EPLF and the "Woyanies" of Tigray, the state and its cadres went to the battle field. Many Christians escaped persecution at that time, by the mercy of God. A commanding officer from Tigray declared, "After we dismiss the enemy on the Northern front, our next target will be to eliminate religion." Sudden death on the battle field did not permit him to fulfill this ambition.

The war in Eritrea and Tigray continued beyond the anticipation of the PMAC compelling the government to accumulate a vast range of arms and manpower. Whenever the Cadres and administrators had to recruit soldiers, they chose religious people and those they hated, hoping they would die in war. The PMAC recruited militia from the streets, schools, and churches by illegal force . When the Cadres came to take young men either to the battle field or to extermination, many mothers living in frustration and awful fear locked their sons in cupboards to hide them. Some of those mothers lost their minds when they found their sons dead from suffocation after the search ended. In the end, the vast accumulation of thieves and vagabonds drafted by the Cadres contributed to their downfall.

CHAPTER TWO

FAILED PROPAGANDA

When the PMAC saw that EPLF and EPRDF controlled all of Wollo, Gojjam, and Shoa provinces, and realized they could possibly capture the capital city, Addis Ababa; they devised a secret plan to start warfare between different peoples and different religions.Though aimed mainly at the Orthodox church and Islams, they included the protestants and meant Tekle's group to be the first victims.

The Military Government set a two-fold campaign against religion and faith, including plans to change large monasteries and churches to museums, to destroy books, clerical robes, and instruments of mass. They planned to incite war between muslims and Christians causing them to fight and lose their jobs, giving the State an excuse to torture them. The State circulated a top secret letter titled: "Religion Is an Obstacle to the Revolution."

Details of the Secret Destroying Decree, quotations from Birhan Family Bulletin. Number 1:

Part One: The Church

1. The more important monasteries and churches should be converted into museums from which the oppressed

masses could draw valuable lessons. The list should include the monasteries and churches of Axum, Debre Damo, Lalibella, Debre Libanos, Zuquala, and the principal monasteries in Gojam, Gondar, Wollo, and important churches in Addis Ababa and Art Galleries.

2. All books of the church written with lame thinking (consciousness) for the exploitation of the feudalists, as Book of the Kings, Book of Mirac, Hymn of Music of Yared, together with books about miracles of saints and the Ark must be confiscated.

3. When the antique treasures of clerical robes found in large monasteries and churches (widespread in the rural areas) are used in the services, they magnify the previous exploitation system and seem to mock the oppressed people. Therefore, all of these materials must be gathered. Some may remain in the country but most should be sent to a friendly country. Where this is not feasible, they should be destroyed.

4. Since the pope in power has limited education and comes from the oppressed class and his educational background is limited, he can therefore be manipulated to become an unwitting instrument for the anti-religious campaign. He has already declared in one sermon that Christ himself propagated socialism. He should be encouraged to elaborate and spread this theme. Priests and church workers who can be depended on to spread the illusion of compatibility between Christianity and Communism should be carefully selected and placed as close to the Patriarch as possible and to preach continually "The message of Christ is Socialism."

5. In addition to measures calculated at weakening the church's independent sources of income, steps should be

taken to restrict the availability, and gradually remove from the market those materials such as wax candles and raisins (used for the making of sacramental wine) required in church services and rituals.

6. Regular church attenders should be identified by a network of informers and systematically discouraged from further attendance by a combination of the following measures: direct offer of monetary incentives, the threat of withdrawal of food ration permits, and loss of jobs.

7. The media must educate the masses by continually ridiculing religion. The propaganda must emphasize:

a. The world we live in is concrete reality and material tasks, and not of spirit and morals as the backward looking reactionaries want us to believe.

b. Religion is always an obstacle to the liberation of oppressed people.

c. Every youth who wants to be a deacon or lay helper must be discouraged and introduced to worldly activities and offered attractive incentives in other careers to prevent followers in the future.

8. To assume that the pseudo-bourgeois who fell through the cracks with the advent of revolution can be saved is a mistake. Consider those who occasionally bowed at a church or a Mosque anti-revolutionaries and kill everyone who has shown a tendency toward a religious belief--whether in churches or homes.

9. Since the power of religion lies in overwhelming the masses with rituals, mystery, and piety, we must tear down the curtain and afflict them. The awe, respect, and moral authority that the clergy and the church inspire must be methodically undermined. Women cadres must pretend to be nuns and go to the monasteries to seduce the monks.

Assign someone to expose the monks' fornication and adultery to the people and frame-up scandals.

10. Invite comrades posing as popes from friendly countries to preach to the priests. Prepare books extolling socialism in the Amharic language for the comrades to give to the priests.

11. Since the Ethiopian clergy are suspicious, the agitation much be arranged with great caution, so the cause does not suffer reproach.

12. The existing effort to foment dissension and divisions among the monks in the Ethiopian Monastery of Jerusalem must continue and be intensified. Increase the number of security guards travelling with pilgrims on pilgrimages because of the large number of monks found in the monasteries of Jerusalem.

Part Two: Moslems

At this time the voice of Islam religions is heard emphatically because of the Arab's wealth and petro-dollars. Even though Moslems are fewer in number among the oppressed mass, yet the former Bourgeois system has exalted them the same as Christianity; both are a barrier to revolution.

Since the sabotage of imperialism strangles the revolution, religious beliefs must be eliminated. Oppression of the Moslems requires a special technic and agitating them must follow a precise plan. It is also advantageous to exploit the historical antagonism between Moslem and Christians to increase conflict between them.

It is necessary to massacre them since they claim the missionaries have organized the Liberation movement in

Eritrea and Wellaga. Those who survive will take vengeance on the Christians.

Tekle and Erkenesh early in their ministry

Country village

People gathering at country church

CHAPTER THREE

DECENCY FOR THE DEAD

Under the Emperor and during the reign of the Derg the Pentecostals suffered the degradation of having no place to bury their dead. The authorities considered a dead Pentecostal no more significant than a dead dog. Older churches refused to share their allotted graveyards, hoping to force the peoples' return to their dead religions.

In a land where embalming is unknown, a body four days dead becomes a serious problem. Often the believers felt compelled to lay the bodies of their departed loved ones in front of the police station or the Coptic Priest's gate to call attention to their plight. The matter did not end with the government forcing someone to unwillingly allow burial in their cemetery. Most likely, a hired person would dig up the body under cover of the night and ring the church bell to awake the people declaring, "The earth spits out the body because their religion is odious and unclean." They will do almost anything to give the church a bad name.

Sometimes, the believers looking for a place to bury their dear ones, would find a desolate area, not part of a farm and the very day of the funeral a local chairman would give the land to a farmer to plow.

In desperation a bereaved family might hire a car to take the body a day's journey and bury it in the countryside; without fail enemies of the truth would call a crowd together to heckle and mock and call down curses on them. Though it is not Ethiopian custom, the family of some of our deceased brothers buried them on their farms. Their neighbors then gathered to insult and belittle the family.

None of these things dismayed God's family. They encouraged themselves in the Spirit understanding that the flesh is only dust; they are willing to accept any abuse for the sake of the Name of Jesus. They delight to have the scriptures fulfilled in their lives, *And ye shall be hated of all men for my name's sake...*(Matthew 10:22). *...in nothing terrified by your adversaries: which is to them an evident token of perdition, but to salvation, and that of God. For unto you it is given in the behalf of Christ, not only to believe on him, but also to suffer for his sake*; (Philippians 1:28,29).

In spite of all these sad scenarios, while the unsaved relatives mourned and wailed and others wrestled for a place to bury the deceased, a few people strong in faith simply laid hands them in the name of Jesus, and the dead stood singing a great song of deliverance! Today, the many churches established through witnessing miraculous resurrections of the dead are filled with strong, undefeated saints.

Because the church increased in amazing numbers, the Security Agency of the Communist Government gave instructions to the five Autonomous Leaders and twenty-five Administrative Regions to give the church graveyards for political reasons. A year before its fall, Tekle received a carbon copy of the decree which helped the church to become legally registered. They can now open an account at the bank in the name of the church--something they could not do before.

Tekle in his office

Bobbye Wendell, widow of Kenneth
Wendell first UPC missionaries to Ethiopia

Grass-roofed country church, mostly
replaced now with iron sheets.

CHAPTER FOUR

IN SPITE OF THE STORMS

The Kenneth Wendell family came as missionaries to Ethiopia in 1969, and the John Harris family joined them in 1970. Before their arrival, Tekle, a well known evangelist in the land, travelled all over the country holding large crusades. He taught holiness, healing, and the in-filling of the Holy Ghost and saw many miracles of deliverance. Though he had pressing invitations to affiliate with other churches, the Lord warned him to wait until the true church came. He met the Wendells, and the Lord confirmed the truth they taught when Bobbye Wendell sent him a tract written by Mike Trepasso. Tekle received an amazing vision with a revelation of baptism in the name of Jesus and Jehovah of the Old Testament is Jesus of the new Testament.

After Brother Wendell baptized him in the Name of Jesus, Tekle witnessed boldly everywhere and baptized Amare, Solomon, Teshome, and others in Addis Ababa. The work that began with lepers living in the cemetery now showed progress reaching out to others, only to be slammed by a series of set-backs arranged by the master of deceit. A confused helper even disfellowshiped Tekle. When John Harris, stationed in Kenya, became Superintendent of Ethiopia, and Brother Freeman, RFS, recognized his leadership ability; they reinstated him.

Tom Fred Tenney, then director of Foreign Missions sent Brother Freeman to Ethiopia in early 1970 to help the Wendells obtain land for a Bible School and finally got the promise of a place on the edge of the desert with perpetual water shortages. Before they could negotiate a change, the Emperor issued that decree against the Pentecostals and ordered the missionaries to leave the country. Persecution accelerated. Brother Tenney hastily sent Brother Freeman on his third trip to Addis Ababa hoping to find a way to avoid deportation of both missionary families. The Emperor refused to see him and the Minister of Education (in charge of church affairs) told him the decree could not be rescinded. As a result he preached the final message in the last legal service held before the decree went into effect.

He recounts, "Broken-hearted, not knowing how to encourage the precious saints in this time of crisis, I walked to the table that served as a pulpit.. Suddenly the Spirit whispered, `One on one.' I told them, `Forget prayer meetings and church services; the decree states if three of you are found with a Bible, you will be thrown in jail and perhaps beaten. That will not help anything. Remember this: the early church operated illegally most of the time, yet it grew.

`Until the dear Lord makes it possible for regular services to begin again, you can go out and win them one at a time. Fast and pray until the Lord leads you to a soul. Even if he or she is unfriendly and doesn't want to hear, hold on to that soul with Christian love until the Holy Ghost falls upon them. Then send him or her to one of the preachers for baptism in the name of Jesus. Do not accompany them; if you don't know when or where the person is baptized the information cannot be beaten out of you.

`I believe the doors will open again, but until then, it's one on one. Remember each one must win one, and encourage the one you win to go out and win another one. Do not let the glorious message die.'"

"I left Ethiopia with a sad heart the next day, praying the God of all grace and comfort to sustain the infant church. Shortly afterward, first the Wendells, and a month later the Harrises had to leave, but, before they left, they arranged over-night erection of a small building from corrugated roofing called the Apostle Peter's School for young children (for a blind). They even concealed a crude plastic-covered baptistery under its dirt floor.

"We preached in many different places in the world for the next two and a half years, and everywhere we requested prayer for the church in Ethiopia. I finally got another visa to visit the beloved land. By this time a communist onslaught on the Empire had the Emperor's back to the wall. He had no time to notice church services by the banned Apostolics.

"I rejoiced to see an overflow crowd in and around the house converted to a church and expressed my joy to Brother Teshome. He answered, `These are the Sunday people, Brother Freeman; another crowd this large gathers here on Saturday. We have no space for all of them to come the same day. When the Emperor declared he would get rid of the Pentecostals, we changed our name to Apostolics, but the communists got rid of the Emperor,'"

This marked the beginning of utter strife and wholesale bloodshed such as few countries have ever known. As the Empire disintegrated, persecution escalated into torture and the communists declared they would destroy the Apostolics.

Tekle receives honorary degree from
Christian Life College, Stockton, CA

CHAPTER FIVE

AMARE'S RETURN

In a time of peril, conflicting rumors, ignorance, misunderstandings, and misguided ambitions coupled with the difficulty Americans had understanding a strange, ancient culture; division blitzed the young church in 1974. Confusion developed during a board meeting with missionary Superintendent John Harris and Missionary Don Ikerd (from Kenya) and Amare walked out followed by several friends.

Tekle and his dear wife Erkenesh felt devastated by the loss of their fellow-laborers and prayed constantly beseeching the Lord to restore unity in His church. After a time, the Lord assured them, "Have patience. One day you will be one flock again."

Though the break-away group took the finance brought by the missionaries to underwrite the expenses of the conference and felt pleased about their possession of the building left by the missionaries, they did not grow and before long the State confiscated the building. the group wrongly thought Tekle and Erkenesh caused all of their problems and reacted with animosity while the blessings of the Lord caused Tekle's church to flourish in the Holy

Ghost.

The group filed a paper with the Intelligence office accusing Tekle as a CIA agent and security personnel followed him everywhere he went. The I.O. blocked the registration of the Apostolic church and issued him a strict warning, "Your church will not be registered and you no longer have the right to preach the Gospel as a licensed preacher."

In spite of harassment and frustration in all the trials this brought them, Tekle and Erkenesh continued to love and pray for those who opposed them. Help came from an unexpected source. When the EPRDF overthrew the military government, all the Intelligence files were either burned or destroyed.

A person who worked in Intelligence and knew Tekle called him, "Brother Tekle, your file is lost; please supply us with the necessary documents to compile a new file for you."

With great joy Tekle took photocopies of lost documents and prepared others that restored his good name and renewed the name of the Apostolic Church of Ethiopia.

After thirteen years, as Erkenesh fasted and prayed, the Lord spoke: *Bring back Amare.* Tekle rejoiced over the word, but others, not sure they wanted Amare back, suggested Erkenesh should fast and pray again. The message came clearly the second time: *Bring back Amare.* After consultation the General Board of the church sent Erkenesh to begin talks on reconciliation with Amare. He welcomed her with humility and tears of joy.

Amare tells his story:

In Arsi Province, Ticho District, Robetown where I was born to a conservative Gurage family, we had only two choices of religion: either Islam or the Orthodox Church (Coptic) where my family worshiped. My mother vowed to St. Mary, "If you will give me a son, I will celebrate a feast in your honor every year and when the boy is grown he will become a priest and serve you."

In childhood I often pretended to be an ark-carrier (an honored position in the Coptic church). I put a piece of wood on my head to represent the ark and covered it with a cloth and designated some of my friends as priests and some as deacons. Part of them followed me and others went before me singing songs as we leaped and danced.

My mother grieved that a so-called holy spring near our home could not be kept clean and reserved for helping people. Moslem shepherds watered their cattle there and made the water unclean. I thought, "When I grow up, I will fence in the spring to keep it holy so its waters can heal the sick." This did not work out. Though I agreed with my mother's plans until I finished the eighth grade, I decided then I could not understand the meaning of religion.

At age twenty I went to work in Awasa on a farm with a man who had strange beliefs. He worshiped only Jesus Christ, would not lie, refused to accept bribes, and lived a clean life--the opposite of my behavior. He had such active faith. He often reasoned with me about my wrong doing; I could not hide anything from him. He would say, "This is sin, and God is not pleased with it."

He made me so uncomfortable, I asked my friends, "Are there other people with these strange ways?" When they said, "No," I wondered who brought this man to me and made plans to change jobs to get away from him. Before I could do anything, he received a good promotion to a better position in another place. Relieved, I thought, "Now I will have rest." But the things he said haunted me.

I liked luxury, having a good time, drinking, parties, and dancing. I tried to stay far away from people with Bibles. I met a cousin in Shashemene and invited him to have a drink with me. He answered, "My faith does not allow me to drink." I got away from him as quickly as possible. But when my work transferred me to Addis Ababa, I stayed at my cousin's home. He invited me to a farewell program for a friend going overseas. What a disappointment to find myself at a church. I thought, "Since I am here, I might as well be patient and listen."

Several blind people came to the platform and sang a special song, I wondered, "How can these men joyfully praise the God who made them blind?" Singing the chorus with them, I realized God has given me good health, but I am the one who is blind because I do not know Him. I made a secret decision to follow Jesus; as we left the meeting I tore up my package of cigarettes and threw them in the sewer.

One of my brothers saw me throw away my package of cigarettes and explained the plan of salvation to me as he understood it. Under his instruction, I was baptized in the name of the Father, Son, and Holy Ghost; received the Holy Ghost; and became a member of the Full Gospel Church. I often witnessed to others how God saved me, then Teshome told me how Brother Teklemariam talked to him about the oneness of the Godhead and baptism in Jesus Name.

One day Teshome said, "We are going to a new place for services."

We found two foreign missionaries and four or five lepers having church; the missionaries touched my heart with their weeping as they prayed. Later, Teshome told them we came because of Tekle's witness. They invited, "Come spend the day with us, and we will study the Word of God together."

They promised that Tekle would be coming soon and we could discuss the scriptures again then. When Tekle came with Solomon Lodamo and taught us, we realized we must not withstand the truth. I reasoned, "Though this lesson is true, I have already been baptized and filled with the Holy Ghost, I will travel in this faith without being baptized in the Name of Jesus."

Tekle took Teshome and Solomon to the river to baptize them, and I went along to watch their clothes as they are baptized. While watching, I heard a voice say distinctly, "When the light is green, vehicles can go forward safely; if they go against the red light, accidents will happen."

As the words came repeatedly, I looked to the right and the left and could see no one. I sat down on the ground and the voice spoke once more, "If you are not baptized in the name of Jesus for the remission of your sins, you are going against the red light."

I sat there in such confusion I did not know when the ceremony ended, but as they started up out of the water, I shouted, "Stop! Stop! I must be baptized." Afterward I testified how God spoke to me.

At the service later that day, Brother Wendell asked me to lead the choruses and I can still remember the powerful anointing of the Holy Ghost that swept over me. Two years later I began to preach the Gospel and Jesus wonderfully multiplied the believers.

Then our enemy, Satan, attacked the infant church twice to destroy it with division. The second time, we suffered many hardships and much agony. When I pondered how it could have happened, the revelation came to me. First, we did not know the scriptural rules and regulations that govern the church; second, we did not realize we should dedicate ourselves totally to keeping the unity of the Spirit.

The church purchased by God with His own blood has its own system of administration operated by the Holy Spirit and all of us must be obedient with a willing spirit and without complaint. We must not add our own ideas, but be obedient with absolute love and respect for our leaders. This will help us reach the desired goal of fruitfulness in the calling of the ministry.

Misunderstandings are inevitable, but those carnal people who gossip and murmur against the things they do not understand confuse the issues and break the unity of the Spirit. Without a desire for conflict, I became a victim of those who aggravated the confusion and fled to escape the problems. Instead of escaping I immersed myself in worse problems and my spiritual life dried up.

A scripture I read over and over sustained me with hope during the thirteen years of separation from my brethren--Daniel 4:34-37:

And at the end of the days I Nebuchadnezzar lifted up mine eyes unto heaven, and blessed the most High and I praised and honored him that liveth for ever, whose dominion is an everlasting dominion, and his kingdom is from generation to generation: And all the inhabitants of the earth are reputed as nothing: and he doeth according to his will in the army of heaven, and among the inhabitants of the earth: and none can stay his hand, or say unto him, what doest thou? At the same time my reason returned unto me; and for the glory of my kingdom, mine honor and brightness returned unto me; and my counsellors and my lords sought unto me; and I was established in my kingdom, and excellent majesty was added unto me. Now I Nebuchadnezzar praise and extol and honor the King of heaven, all whose words are truth, and his ways judgment: that those that walk in pride he is able to abase.

In the twelfth year of our separation from the church I became seriously ill and despaired of life. Abebach, my wife, sought help for me and could find none. I wept, realizing I had no brethren who would come visit us and pray for me as I hung on the verge of death. God in His great mercy spared my life.

I did not shed tears in vain, for exactly one year later Sister Erkenesh came to our home, "God sent me to help you return to the fold. Let us forget the disappointments of the past and become one again. Jesus tells me there are good things ahead for you if you are obedient. What is your answer?"

"Who am I to refuse a message from the Lord?" I replied, "I am ready to do His will."

After the second visit she brought me to Brother Tekle and the elders of the church. They accepted me with brotherly love and with the Spirit of God. Brother Tekle encouraged me with many kind words, "Now, you can work for Jesus with spiritual liberty. If in our separation we have accomplished a great work for Jesus, we will see how wonderfully He will help us in our unity."

This amazing reconciliation in the church astonished not only the saints in the church but also the outsiders. I cannot easily explain how the Lord has moved me by the Holy Spirit to seek Him and serve Him wholeheartedly. Now, I understand church government and the sweet communion of the Holy Ghost. My life is a lesson and a triumphant testimony showing how leaders of the church can have a wide heart and be led by the Holy Ghost to restore those who fall by the way. Though one has made mistakes and been denounced, let no one say, "This case is hopeless; neither prayer nor words will help." Jesus is able to restore with prayer, holy love, and wisdom those who have missed the road.

Amare and Ayele eating Ethiopian food

CHAPTER SIX

SOLOMON'S TESTIMONY

No matter how strong, prayerful, and distinguished a preacher may seem to be, there is no abundant life outside the church of the Living God. As trillions of cells make up the human body, so each of us is a cell in the body of Christ. A second body cannot be found in the scripture. Since coming back to the church, I clearly understand that to be disfellowshiped from the church means to die a spiritual death. Looking back to those desolate years apart from the body brings me shivers from hell.

As one of the first converts to the true Gospel, I fell in love with the truth. I had a good job with many benefits such as free boat excursions, extensive travel, and holiday bonuses, but when my faith in Jesus Christ cost me my job, I counted its advantages as nothing and cherished the truth.

The Lord gave me utmost spiritual joy, true apostolic love. We enjoyed a great oneness of spirit among our brethren. Jesus provided for all of my needs, and living, working, and moving in the church seemed like paradise to me. Our brothers and sisters fulfilled the scripture in John 15:12: *This is my commandment, that ye love one another, as*

I have loved you.

Little by little, our first love began to diminish. We doubted each other's sincerity, and suspicion grew unnoticed among the brethren. Leaders in Addis Ababa began questioning those in Awasa and other provinces. We put each other's motives under careful scrutiny, and soon division and strife fractured our fellowship. The whole group acted the same as other unredeemed denominations. In the following days, deprived of Apostolic love, we came together to question ourselves. We even set days of fasting and prayer and experienced temporary and tentative joy afterward, but never lasting joy or true refreshing of our spirits.

During this time, I became a high school teacher in another province. I witnessed with all my might and started a small chapel-like meeting. We had a thread-like, scanty, outward show of unity among our preachers, but the tares of doubts and suspicion remained. False laughter and false love prevailed among believers with true love, the most important thing, missing.

This situation brought tragedy: five disfellowshiped preachers came to tell me about this new development and without seeking an explanation, I immediately took their side and joined them in a concerted attack on the other group. From that time I led in bringing heavy accusations against innocent brothers and sisters and wounded many souls. I antagonized them wherever I met them and preached against them from many pulpits. If it had been possible, I would have swallowed them alive.

It is difficult for me to recount all that I said and did in my assault on the church. Since it will not edify the reader, allow me to hide my wrongs in the deep waters of the tears I shed when I came to myself. I wept for days and months. With a heart full of sorrow, I repented of all my evil words and came back to the church after thirteen years. I felt like a thief and could not look the saints in the eyes. Sleep went away from my eyes in the night. I asked forgiveness of everyone and after a ten day fasting-prayer session began to feel peace. I took another ten day for fasting and prayer, taking only a little tap water. Now I am alive and refreshed! My first love is fully restored and I bask in the sweet spirit of oneness in the church. Blessed be the wonderful name of Jesus; He has washed me with His blood once more! Now I know I will inherit the Kingdom of God.

Before the thirteen years of strife and division that culminated in the preachers being disfellowshiped, I had several positions and felt the great grace of the Lord in everything I did. I led the singing and preached, served as an ordained deacon and as secretary of the church board. Almost all the English preaching reached the ears of the saints by my interpreting. When I joined the disfellowshiped group, I lost all that grace. My heart felt empty. We fasted and prayed during those years, but I did not feel apostolic love, unity of spirit, or joy of the Holy Ghost in my daily life. My Christian experiences sank back to the level of denominational times.

Please hear my solemn words, dear disfellowshiped brother or sister, run back to your pastor or leader and ask forgiveness. Don't let the sun set on your situation. Go back to your Father's house and excuse yourself with deep repentance. The road out of the church certainly leads to hell.

You may think as we did--you have a church, even after you are cut off (and it is never without a cause). To some extent you are blessed, but do not be deceived. Mind you, it is only a shadow of the True Church of the Living God. Being a shadow you have only an artificial church divorced from reality. In the first place, there is only one church, one body, and one God. Jesus will not establish His church on strife and division.

Listen! dear Church, please leave the doors open for those who come back with full repentance. I am so grateful my church left the doors open for me to enter when I returned. Had I been discouraged or received with anything other than apostolic love, they would have doomed me to eternal death. Because of my church's mercy I am alive spiritually. Now, *I can do all things through Christ which strengthenth me.* (Philippians 4:13).

By the mercy of Jesus Christ,
Solomon Lodamo

Solomon (right) with Amare and his wife

CHAPTER SEVEN

ASHENAFI ANDARGE

It is hard for thee to kick against the pricks (Acts 9:5).

I remember the accepted day of my salvation in 1970 when Brother Teklemariam baptized me in the deep waters of Lake Awasa for the remission of my sins and I received the Holy Ghost. When I arose after burying the old Adam and becoming one with Christ by putting on His living body, the power of the resurrection and the joy of the Holy Ghost became greater in my soul than words could express. I must say thanks be unto God for His unspeakable gift.

When the call came to preach this true gospel, I accepted it without hesitation. The God who separated me from my mother's womb and saved me by His grace made me ready to go. My faithful God did not repent of His grace and the call; He took care of me from the day I obeyed Him. I lost nothing. He helped me advance my ministry along with other brothers.

However, we did not understand the secret of subjection to the leaders of the living church of God which led to my suspension from the ministry for an unlimited period of time. I did not accept instruction and continued preaching outside the church where God cannot be found, and He refused to cooperate with me.

I transgressed the divine commandment that says, *Touch not mine anointed and do my prophets no harm.* I spoke against the church and the men of God to the saints to cause them to abandon the mother church and be lost. I feel sad when I remember my foolish efforts to disintegrate the works of those who brought us the church.

The servants of the living God who brought us the good news of salvation are messengers of the church and representatives of Christ's glory; therefore, we must show them great respect and serve with them in humility. We cannot oppose men who are anointed of God and be blessed. We see how the Lord worked through men in the olden times and the Word makes plain we can be successful and prosper if we believe in God and His prophets:

...Jehosaphat stood and said, hear me, O Judah, and ye inhabitants of Jerusalem; Believe in the Lord your God, so shall ye be established, so shall ye prosper (II Chronicles 20:20).

Saul did not understand the secret of God's anointing oil on the man of His choice and turned against David. But David understood the holy anointment and refused to lift his hand against Saul, even when the Lord put him at his feet. Because Saul opposed both David and Samuel, the anointed prophet, he finally perished in his folly on Mount Gilboa by the hands of his enemies. I Samuel 31:2-6.

When I considered these things, I had no alternative but to return to the church with my saints. The church accepted me with absolute mercy and forgiveness and allows me to continue my ministry with the blessing of the living church of God. Now, I serve my God with full and free salvation under Jesus Christ, the true shepherd of one flock. Blessed and hallowed be His name for ever and ever!

Finally, to all of you members of the United Pentecostal Church International world wide who may read my testimony. Please understand there is no salvation outside the church. To dwell peaceably in the house of the Lord is your life. Allow me to remind you in the name of our Lord Jesus Christ to serve your leaders.

Blessed are they that dwell in thy house: they will still be praising thee. Selah. For a day in thy courts is better than a thousand. I had rather be a doorkeeper in the house of my God, than to dwell in the tents of the wicked (Psalms 84:4,10).

Rejoice

Ayele, Amare, and Tekle at Tekle's house

Revival at Somali Border

CHAPTER EIGHT

AS I REMEMBER...

By WOLDEGIORGIS

My beginnings go back to Wollo Province, Yeju district, Gubalafto sub-district and the Famel locale where my parents attended the Orthodox church. Illiterate farmers, they did not understand the value of education for their children. When I got old enough to care for our cattle, the wonder of God's world around me inspired in my heart a longing for knowledge.

I enrolled in the local church school and studied all the books they offered including some which delved into mysteries of the Trinity and other matters. When the church gave me a book rewarding faithful attendance, 1 learned for the first time about the three divisions of Christianity into Catholic, Orthodox, and Protestant. This troubled me.

"Which of these three came first and which is the true church? When did Christianity begin?" I asked, but the religious teachers could not answer. I studied Geez and poetry seeking knowledge and finally came to Addis Ababa in 1960. I wandered to many different monasteries trying to find answers but no one could enlighten me. I became so discouraged with Christianity, I decided to learn magic and sorcery; because God loved me He did not allow me success in this effort.

Holding a book called Angel Satanael (Lucifer), I went to the River Akaki one morning to call the devils. As I read the demons came out of the water and threw me into the deepest part. In acute danger of drowning I wanted to call on God, but I have quarrelled with him. At last I cried, "O God of my father and mother, help me!" Immediately, in His mercy, He brought me to safety.

I met the Norwegian missionaries in 1966 and they gave me a Bible; later I met Evangelical preachers who convinced me of the evil of my books on magic and sorcery so I burned them. The Norwegian Mission sent me to Negele Borena for education. I received academic schooling, but no answer to my questions. By then I had another question. If God is trinity (three persons), which one made me?

I met Evangelist Teklemariam in the summer of 1967. I marvelled at this independent preacher who, without funds, preached with power and great boldness. He touched my heart; I liked his style of preaching and I started following him everywhere he held services. Though he could not at that time define the first religion, he declared strictly, "You must believe in Jesus Christ, repent, and be baptized with the Holy Ghost to receive power."

His words encouraged me and I followed his example of kneeling in prayer. I based my prayer on the lady in Mark 7:25-30 who begged for crumbs of mercy; I begged for Apostolic crumbs of knowledge.

The mission sent me to Awassa in 1969 to learn

church history and Bible. Tekle took me to his home to meet his family. On November 1, 1969, while I knelt with them in prayer, the Lord heard my heart's cry and gloriously filled me with the Holy Ghost.. I sang a song in the Spirit saying, "I want to proclaim Thy salvation." A voice replied, "Stand and proclaim in Borena."

Though I did not fully understand, I went to Borena for a week. On my return I brought my questions to the Bible School.

"Is the word *trinity* in the Bible?"

"What is the difference between baptism in the the titles in Matthew 28:19 and baptism in the name of Jesus in Acts 2:38?"

"Where was the Son and the Holy Ghost when God created the heaven and earth?"

My queries brought a storm of opposition and they quickly expelled me from the school.

By the time I returned to Tekle's house in February 1970, the Wendell's ministry had led him into the truth that has transformed thousands of lives in Ethiopia. With many scriptures he proved to me the oneness of God and baptism in the name of Jesus as practiced by the Apostles. I immediately requested baptism in the Bible way and found the long-desired rest for my soul.

I discussed my call to the ministry with Brother Tekle and went first to Dilla where the Lord gave me many souls. Tekle and his wife Erkenesh and I ministered in Awassa, Wolaytta, Kembatta, and Addis Ababa. Great revival came. We explained with zeal and anointing the perfection of the apostle's faith to the religious people bound by tradition.

Many believed and were baptized, and we left them

to take the gospel to others wherever we felt like going. We did not understand how to establish a church or to teach its spiritual discipline, but, for His name sake, Jesus honored the true Gospel we preached and saved souls.

After a year in Sidamo, the Lord led me to Nazareth. I had not been there before and knew no one and had no money for the journey. A few brothers pooled their small change for my bus fare and Tekle gave me twenty-five copies of his book *Divine Power* to sell. After reaching Nazareth I went to Brother Bekele Madebo's house in Wonji Town and witnessed for a week before I went to Kuriftu. Sister Sophia Asfaw gave me a place to stay and I continued preaching in that area.

All of the ministers received a call to attend a meeting in Addis Ababa in April 1971. Each of us explained our call and received a preacher's license in accordance. A board was formed with Brother Wendell as superintendent. We did not understand the significance of the headquarters church and other branches, the board and the superintendent's authority, nor our ministerial responsibilities. Without training we simply said, "I am called; now send me so I can go and preach His Word wherever I want to go." We labored like a bee flitting here and there without a queen.

We had no knowledge of the formalities of the church as taught by Paul in Acts 20:28: *Take heed therefore unto your selves and to all the flock, over the which the Holy Ghost hath made you overseers, to feed the church of God, which he hath purchased with his own blood.*

1 Corinthians 12:25:*That there should be no schism in the body; but that the members should have the same care one for another.*

We simply operated on emotions and imagination which caused many problems. Sad misunderstandings between leaders combined with lack of judgement developed tragic and unnecessary persecution that caused the death of Brother Tekle's small son Moses. I saw myself as a peacemaker and tried to mediate between brethren until I received an embarrassing letter that accused me of being a trouble maker. I stopped trying to mediate and gave myself to serious prayer; however, before we could resolve the problem, Brother Wendell was forced by the government to leave the country.

The work of the Gospel stopped everywhere and the Holy Ghost did not fall as before because we no longer enjoyed oneness of accord. The brethren in Addis Ababa suffered persecution. The police arrested Brother Worku Gebremariam in St. Trinity. Brother Amare and others suffered the tension of confusion, and Brother Nigussie Haile was imprisoned in Wollayta. Generally the recently founded Apostolic Church of Ethiopia fell into serious problems from 1972 until 1974.

Though we did not understand the foundation and the authority of the church, we felt burdened for the disintegration of the work and sadness for the cold spirited slackening of preaching the Gospel of Jeusus Christ.. When saints who suffered to maintain unity asked us *why* we had no answer.

Then Jesus led me to Sister Yewubdar Abebe's house the same day her sister Kelemua came to visit. Through prayer and counsel with Mama Worke, the Lord gave us a plan. Mama Worke and Sister Yewubdar went to Brother Tekle with advice and I went to Brother Amare. Success crowned out efforts! On April 12, 1974 we gathered in

Mama Solome Gebrestatiyos's house under Sister Yewubdar's leadership. We resolved the problems and made a firm decision to work together in the future and to preach the Gospel we have accepted with one heart. We formed a temporary committee to help us elect a pastor who could lead the church with full responsibility.

We shamed Satan by preparing Articles of Faith with a renewed Spirit. This effort caused the Gospel to go out again widespread with liberty. In September we assembled and elected Brother Tekle Superintendent of the Apostolic Church of Ethiopia and Brother Amare his assistant. We gathered together the saints dispersed and scattered for three years and rented a house for a place of worship. As we worked together with one heart, new souls came in and the work went forward in Nazareth and Wonji. We reached out to Arsi Province and started branches in Assela, Dera, and Cholie.

Though renewed in heart and love, we did not have the church's administration manual and did not know the roles and responsibilities of the superintendent, presbyters, and sectional leaders. This gave the enemy an opportunity to sow discord again.

Because of disobedience and misunderstandings between preachers, we met frequently to solve these problems with common understanding. We met May 22, 1975 in Addis Ababa with representatives of the United Pentecostal Church International, Rev. John Harris and Rev. Donald Ikerd, missionaries from Kenya sent to assist us. Since we did not understand parliamentary procedures the meeting became noisy and we refused to listen to each other. At last, without waiting for final decisions the following preachers walked out of the assembly hall, Amare Waktola,

Teshome Gebre, Nigussie Haile, Worku Gebremariam, Ashenafi Andarge and Woldegiorgis Sisay. We received a letter afterwards saying we are disfellowshiped from the ministry because of pride and disobedience.

Because we had not learned the authority of the church, we said defiantly, "God created us and called us, though men may say we cannot preach, we will preach anyway."

We made our decision to work outside the unity of the church ignoring this scripture:.

Verily I say unto you, whatsoever ye shall bind on earth shall be bound in heaven: and whatsoever ye shall loose on earth shall be loosed in heaven (Matthew 18:18).

The words of Jesus began working on us and did not allow us to go free. In the period of separation from the church, things went all right for three years, though my brothers blamed me for my previous efforts to make peace.

They denounced me bitterly saying, "You brought us into danger saying peace and unity."

Their words made me sad, but I could not feel condemned for following the leading of the Holy Ghost.

In our determination to work in one accord, we forgot the Word of God in 1 Corinthians 12:28: *And God hath set some in the church, first apostles, secondarily prophets, thirdly teachers, after that miracles , then gifts of healings, helps, governments, diversities of tongues.*

And John 20:23: *Whose soever sins ye remit, they are remitted unto them; and whose soever sins ye retain, they are retained.*

We did not have success.

In 1976 we rented a big warehouse in Addis Ababa, Merkto section for our church services. We got land in

Nazareth and started construction of a church. We organized choirs, the youth, and the women to work for the Lord. As the sheep tied with a long rope thinks she is free, the rope will not allow her to go where she will.

Brother Ashenafi Andarge spoke to some of the brothers and sisters secretly and the next thing we knew, the church in Nazareth is closed and they have all gone back to the headquarters church. We were too angry to evaluate if this action is from God or from Satan. We accused Brother Tekle of plotting against us and wrote many letters and accusations against him to various government offices for vengeance. We had no success and nothing we did changed the will of God nor hindered the Church bound to Jesus Christ.

Matthew 16:19 reads: *Again I say unto you, That if two of you shall agree on earth as touching any thing that they shall ask, it shall be done for them of my Father which is in heaven.*

And Matthew 28:20 declares, *Teaching them to observe all things whatsoever I have commanded you: and lo, I am with you alway, even unto the end of the world.*

These words witnessed against us and we remained empty handed. This time of severe temptations brought back the diseases that plagued me before my conversion and the doctor could not cure me. God did not refuse me food, but my bound spirit denied me the refreshing of the Word and spiritual nourishment. I found idleness difficult so I took employment in a bank and began attending night school to pass the time until Jesus turned his face toward me again.

In 1981 I visited the saints in Assela, and on my return the Lord impressed me with Matthew 5:25,26: *Agree with tine adversary quickly, whiles thou art in the way with him; lest at any time the adversary deliver thee to the judge, and the judge deliver thee to the officer, and thou be cast into prison. Verily I say unto thee, Thou shalt by no means come out thence till thou hast paid the uttermost farthing.*

The words shocked me and I trembled. I felt confused and wanted to say, "Let us return to the church," but I remembered the arrows thrown at me in 1971-72 and in 1975. I wanted to evade the scripture, but I feared its message. In the meantime some of the saints asked me, "You evangelists taught us to love one another, yet you dispute with each other and separate yourselves. Why do you not become reconciled." I had no answer.

Brother Dejene Segu came to my home several times pleading with me to return to the church, but I refused. Later I heard that the Spirit of the Lord spoke through Amare Waktola at a prayer meeting at Brother Moges' house. This made me happy remembering how they opposed the unity before.

I went to see Brother Ejigu Moges when I heard that he lay sick at his mother's house in Nazareth. He asked me to explain the beginning of the church and how the division came. After I told him the whole story he answered, "Why didn't you wait until the meeting finished before you left? This is the work of the flesh, and you are still responsible."

We agreed to pray together, hoping for an answer from the Lord.

I went to see Amare and others in Addis Ababa, hoping for a change of heart, but they said, "We have cleansed our hearts of hatred, but we will stay as we are until Jesus tells us to unite with those we left."

I returned home feeling sad and earnestly prayed again for the Lord to lead me.

Meanwhile my studies helped me get a better job at the Transport Corporation, relieving my mind of worries about daily needs, but I had no rest in my heart. When I prayed I reasoned with God, "Lord, when you brought me to this place, didn't you promise to supply my needs, make me fruitful in your service and bless me? Where are the promises? Did I come here only to benefit the flesh? My heart cries out to see the fruit of the Gospel". My only relief came as I met with Brother Ejigu Moges twice a week to pray for the Gospel to be preached freely in unity.

Material I was responsible for at work got stolen, and Sisters Yewubdar and Kelemua came to comfort me. As we shared our mutual concern for the church we felt led to arrange a meeting with good-spirited Brother Worku and Brother Moges in February 1985. When I told them how God frequently warned me with Matthew 18:23-25, they confirmed the Lord gave all five of us the same message and we felt we must do something about it. We agreed that each of us must contact the separated saints in different places (as decided) and we would meet again once a month in Debrezeit to pray and plan.

When I spoke to Dejene Segu, he arranged a meeting with Brother Tekle and Sister Erkenesh at his home in Nazareth and restoration came through the understanding of the leaders. The scattered saints in Addis returned through the efforts of Brother Worku. In a short time everyone but Amare, Solomon, and Negussie came back to the fold. We held fast to hope that they would rejoin us one day.

All of us who returned decided to live and work for unity with brotherly love in the church according to the Word of God. Since I am called to be a minister, I followed the advice of my church, and began to work with Brother

Dejene with one heart and one spirit in the Eastern and Southern section. God has blessed us richly and multiplied the work. In '85 we baptized seventy three people, the next year one hundred eighty-six, and the following years, at least five hundred a year. I have been ordained and am the leader of Debrezeit sub-sections. I am happy, serving my Lord with gladness and above all I am thankful for the leaders of the church who accepted me with a pure spirit and full forgiveness enabling me to live and work in the love of God.

Had it not been for their Christlike acceptance and the love of the saints, we would still be bound with the curse. Today I refuse to listen to malicious words that would bring antagonism in the church for I know the Lord works only with love. I pray the Lord's richest blessing on Brother Dejene and Sister Menbre because they helped me both before and after my return to church. They advise and comfort me in my ministry and in my personal life.

If every minster would pay attention, respect, and be in one accord with his fellow ministers, then the work of God could move forward with full strength and the Holy Ghost would be poured out abundantly everywhere. If we had worked together like we do now for the past twelve years, the gospel of Jesus Christ would have filled Ethiopia and flooded the neighboring countries.

A MESSAGE TO MINISTERS

I have a message for the servants of God. After Jesus established the church by His blood, He set in the church apostles, prophets, preachers of the gospel, helps, and governments (administration), I Corinthians 12:28. All of us are given grace as servants of the church--not independent owners--but hired by God. We understand we must look to Jesus who bought us with His precious blood on the cross. According to Jude, those who separate themselves are fruitless trees, on whom God will execute judgement. If we offend the church it would be better for us to have a mill stone tied to our neck and be cast into the sea (Mark 9:42).

During the time we did not understand this ministry, we fed many people non-edifying words that destroyed many. We faced much suffering, many hardships, lost our saints, saw our work burnt by fire, and remained fruitless. We thank God for His abundant mercy that has restored to us peace and rest for our conscience instead of vengeance for the destruction we caused.

Preacher means servant, not property owner. The shepherd must feed and protect the sheep and he will receive his wages at the appointed time by his Employer. If he ignores his responsibility, fails to feed the sheep, or sells them or exposes them to wild beasts; he will be accused of spoiling God's property instead of receiving wages.

Therefore, ye shepherds, hear the Word of the Lord; As I live, saith the Lord God, surely because my flock became a prey, and my flock became meat to every beast of the field, because there was no shepherd, neither did my shepherds search for my flock, but the shepherds fed themselves, and fed not my flock...thus saith the Lord God; Behold I am against the shepherds; and I will require my flock at their hand, and cause them to cease from feeding the flock; neither shall the shepherds feed themselves anymore, for I will deliver my flock from their mouth, that they may not be meat for them (Ezekiel 35:7,8,10).

We feel sad for the unfaithful pastors who lost their flocks and their works are burned with fire.

And the Lord said, who then is that faithful and wise steward, whom his Lord shall make ruler over his household, to give them their portion of meat in due season (Luke 13: 41-46).

Pastors who follow their own arrogant ideas damage the unity of the church. God will restore His church but the misguided preacher will fail. We need to learn from Absalom who stole the hearts of Israel with smooth words. Many innocent people died with the deceiver. Note Paul's word to Timothy in I Timothy 3:15: *But if I tarry long, that thou mayest know how thou oughtest to behave thyself in the house of God, which is the church of the living God, the pillar and ground of the truth.*

Church built as a result of a boy raised from the dead. Twelve churches converted and joined us

Brothers Bekele, Tekle, Ayele, Ezekiel,
Getechew, and Dejene on a trip to Israel

Bobbye Wendell and Addis Ababa
preachers

CHAPTER NINE

RELIGIOUS CONSPIRACY

Tekle explains: After the Derg came to power, the fanatic young communists who lit the revolutionary flame focused on religion. they planned to kill everyone over forty years old and to sweep religious people out of the country. They forced the missionaries who brought different kinds of religion to Ethiopia to leave the land. This enhanced the apostolic church's opportunity for growth and abundant chances to go fearlessly through many open doors.

The preachers employed with salaries by missionaries abandoned their flocks and took jobs as communist cadres to persecute religion for 400 Birr a month. The missionaries who brought the money took it back with them to their own lands. When the problems and confusion relaxed somewhat, many of them returned to find they had only buildings; their former saints are now members of the Apostolic church.

From that time those leaders started conspiring against me. They bribed district administrators and police commissioners to kill me, but every effort failed. it is not possible to destroy a person that God protects. a long time has passed since they sentenced me to death.

As time passed and more of their saints came daily to the Apostolic church, they held a meeting conspiring against me. Two hot-tempered men volunteered to murder me with a knife. But as they approached they saw the angel of the Lord standing by me with a drawn sword in his hand. When He rebuked them, they fell on their knees in repentance and today they are good, faithful servants of the Lord.

Psalms 34:7: *The angel of the Lord encampeth round about them that fear him, and delivereth them.*

These words have brought us deliverance many times. Over and over we have seen supernatural deliverance wrought by God's ministering army who protect us and work against the evil doers.

Religious leaders hired killers and thieves to harass us. They broke in the roof of our church, but it did not stop a flood of their people coming to us nor stop the angel's smiting them.

After EPRDF came to power and we had religious freedom, they saw they could not win the people with the Bible. Fearing to lose more people, ten organizations came together to fight us, even to beating the people with rods. But the government understood their conspiracy and warned them in public meetings in Awassa and Ambo.

Pastors of a church in Melge Wondo disobeyed the warning from the government and terrorized the church with a fusillade of shots. When the saints came out, they beat and severely wounded both men and women, but the government and outsiders stood with us against them. The next day a large number of their members and their choirs denounced the deeds of their leaders and came to us. We saw that Romans 8:28 is still true: *All things work together for good.*

We found their conspiracy useful in spreading the work of the Lord mightily.

Members of these opposing churches who worked in public offices hid our files and misread our cases so we could not get our requests answered. They delayed our applications for graveyards, permits for church construction, and kindergartens. Cases that should have been completed in a week suffered four years of delays in their hands. After EPRDF removed these people from office, we received prompt attention.

THE SORCERS' EFFORTS

When our opponents saw that we multiplied daily, the spirit of Balaam fell upon them. They hired Balaams to put curses on us. For one conference they spent much money on wizards and magicians to cause thunderstorms and snow to interrupt the services. They stayed on a hilltop from the beginning to the end with their hands alternately stretched out toward us and toward heaven. Nothing happened, the greatly blessed conference ended with no interruptions.

As Balaam declared in Leviticus 23, *How shall I curse, whom God has not cursed?* Neither the gates of hell nor enchanters and diviners can prevail against the church.

In Sidamo Wara 130,000 people assembled for a conference. The hired sorcers and wizards magic number is nine, so they met together nine times and slaughtered nine big bulls to stop all conferences in the region. Dismayed they read the signs of the fat in the animals stomachs and told those who hired them, *The churches will win and they will hold conferences here every year.* All the wizards and diviners acknowledged defeat and said farewell to the area.

They left the place forever.

When the persecutors in Butajera failed to abolish our religion, they consulted with famous, much trusted wizards and asked them to destroy us with their magic. They answered, "They have a mighty God, so you cannot challenge them, but you will not die if you do not oppose them."

They did not listen and continued their strong opposition against us and in three months time thousands of people died of a strange disease that resembled malaria. None of the saints contracted the illness and from that time people feared to come against us.

When all the attempts at sorcery failed, our opponents devised a new plan to prevent their members coming to us. In night services they put reflective white cloth robes on four men and spot-lighted them with a large flashlight, announcing to their members, "The angels have come, let us rejoice with loud voices."

This succeeded three times before the police found the men rehearsing in the jungle and exposed the farce. Disgusted, many of the people came to the true gospel.

CHAPTER TEN

LET THE REDEEMED SAY SO

by TEKLE

My family and I have been miraculously spared by God's wonderful hand of protection many times. I recount these to give all glory and honor to the holy name of Jesus. when a problem or a disease comes to our house, no one fears. Even our children have learned to accept whatever happens. It is good to accept any circumstance. If a member of our family is sick, we believe he will be healed by prayer. No one worries that the sick one will die. If fear and disease integrates, one does not escape death, for fear is a trap. We believe God!

When I was a young child, enemies threw me in a flooded river twice. Each time it took so long to find a swimmer to rescue me; all hope for my survival failed. Just as my family and friends started to mourn my death, life returned to my body.

While playing, my childhood friends and I put many bullets in the fire. Though we stood near, when the explosion came nothing touched me by a miracle of God.

A typhoid epidemic struck my village and so many people died; not enough people remained alive to bury the dead. The wild animals ate the dead. In our house only one child died, but we all looked like skeletons. After I recovered, I went for a walk one night and a hyena ran between my legs and took me to the bush. I fell off and sat on the ground face to face with the hyena. Then the Lord gave me wisdom and still looking at the hyena, I started sliding backward on my buttocks; he slid the same way toward me. When I reached home I yelled "Help!" loudly and the hyena backed up a little giving me a chance to jump up and run in the house. This made him so mad he dug up the ground all around the house with his paws before he finally left.

One day, I climbed a tree over forty-five feet tall, and stepped on a rotten limb causing me to fall to the ground. God not only saved my life, but I had no broken bones.

I cracked my whip with all my strength once on a hillside. It curled around a tree stump and a dead branch pierced my stomach. They carried me home, thinking I could not live with such a big stick in my belly, but when they pulled it out, God's healing power let me live.

Even before we came to life-giving faith, Jesus relieved Erkenesh of dental problems and healed her of cerebral malaria.

Through the testimony of a young boy, God healed me of a severe intestinal disease that caused me much pain for twelve years.

Led by the Lord, I left Awassa just before a population of six thousand people came to slaughter me. Hoping to prevent my escape they set up check points and closed all of the roads leading out of the town, declaring that anyone who found me should kill me. They killed my son, but Jesus arranged my escape.

In Debrezeit, most of the town's population broke up a prayer meeting and beat me with a big rod with nails in it. They half scalped me and I lay in a coma for a week, but Jesus healed me.

A poisonous lowland snake bit me, but the Lord dispelled the poison in my body and I was made whole.

Murderers with knives surrounded my wife and me in a house in Negelle. God prevented them from action though they stayed until 3:00 A.M. We escaped at 5:00 A.M. by His mercy.

A demon in the form of a man came to torture me to death, but an angel in a white garment revealed the man's true identity and told me to say repeatedly, "In Jesus name". That lovely name delivered me and I escaped from Satan's hand.

My daughter Jerusalem lay critically ill with malaria for nine days and died. I prayed to the Lord of the resurrection with hope and after two hours, her life returned.

When we began in the gospel work, the believers did not understand that tithing is compulsory and we suffered many hardships. Since Mehret, our oldest daughter did not receive the proper nutrition she needed as a small child, she developed a nagging cough that lasted for ten years. We rebuked the cough in the name of Jesus and it went away, never to return.

Boiling water accidently spilled on Eyosyas' hand and the doctor feared he had lost the use of it permanently; we firmly held on to God in prayer and he received complete healing with full use of his hand.

An officer under Emperor Haile Selasse signed my death sentence, but my would-be killers perished in the revolution.

Abraham contacted an intestinal disease that held on until we lost hope; then Jesus gave his life back.

A man put his machine gun on my chest and pulled the trigger, but the bullet did not fire; I was spared.

Planning to shoot me in the head, an enemy of the gospel lay in ambush; the bullet only fanned my hair.

I suffered severe asthma for three years and it disappeared through prayer. Thirteen years I have been free from asthma by the power of Jesus. I had painful attacks of sinus for ten years before the Lord delivered me.

Returning from school with Eyasu, Erkenesh's younger brother ran ahead. He looked back to see an enemy strangling Eyasu with his own scarf until his eyes bulged dangerously near death. The young man ran back; the attacker released Eyasu and wanted to run away, but Erkenesh's brother grabbed him and bear him severely.

A very devoted mother in our church has a demon possessed son. One day Satan told him to get a knife and kill Jerusalem, our daughter. he bought a sharp knife and came to the church compound only to learn Jerusalem had gone to town. He thought, "If I can't kill her, I will kill one of the other preachers' children." He saw Brother Worku's son and pretended to be friendly until he got him out of the church compound and stabbed him in the stomach, but not too deeply. The boy held his hand over the wound to protect himself and before someone rescued the lad, his hand received severe stab wounds which healed with treatment. He drank the cup meant for Jerusalem, but Jesus helped him.

After the Derg came to power, they corrupted the

young people, often stealing young girls and putting them in the army. Since going to school became too dangerous for Mehret, a spiritual girl, we had no choice but arrange marriage for her at age sixteen. A good and obedient girl, she agreed to marry the godly young man we chose for her. Her husband is a preacher of the gospel and they now have three children.

I developed diabetes after a long preaching journey where I drank only soft drinks because safe drinking water could not be found. When I consulted a doctor, my blood sugar had reached 400. This condition persisted for a while, before the Name of Jesus healed me completely.

After a missionary trip to West Africa, I developed yellow fever and lay unconscious for thirty-five days. Despair for my life prevailed; my pancreas swelled to the extremity; but with hope gone, Jesus the healer touched me and restored my health.

Eyosyas, our oldest son went to Kenya Bible School for a year, then Brother Church in Canada offered to sponsor him at the Bible School there and Brother David Ward helped him to go. He stayed two years and graduated.

I attended a conference at New Orleans in the USA. On Saturday as I attempted to open the door to a restaurant, the large plate glass above it fell and cut my leg in several places. One cut above my knee went to the bone. The doctor who stitched it told me to stay in bed, but I hobbled to the Sunday night service. Brother Jack Cunningham called me forward and as he and thousands of others prayed for me, the power of Jesus Christ touched me and I danced all over the platform. When I went to the doctor the next day to have the stitches removed he scolded me for waiting until the wound completely dried before I came!

In the meantime, the school attended by Abraham and Jerusalem sank to such depths of immorality they suffered constant danger. Boys armed with knives demanded money and submission from them and threatened their lives. When Abraham got seriously hurt defending Jerusalem, we knew something had to be done. We contacted Brothers Haney and Rash in Stockton, California, USA asking that they keep our children in school there until the scene changed in Ethiopia. We felt pleased for good progress in their education. Later, they went to stay at Tupelo, Mississippi in the Children's mansion under the kind direction of Brother Steve Drury and his wife.

Since Erkenesh's longing for her children made her sick, we decided to bring all three of them home. Though we rejoiced to have our children with us again, we faced a serious problem with their schooling. Many school officials wanted big bribes and if they sat for entry examinations, they would not allow them to pass. Erkenesh then cried, "Why did I bring them back?" The distress caused her to suffer a stroke and the right side of her body became paralyzed. She lay seriously ill for seven days before the power of prayer raised her up.

Later, we went to a lowland place and Erkenesh wore boots, when she removed the right boot, her leg became contorted with a hard cramp from her waist down. After three days of suffering, prayer in the name of Jesus prevailed.

When we went for a funeral in Wonji Shoa, a place noted for extremely hot climate, she took a shower and the doctor later said the blood drained from her head, and, again, her right side paralyzed. He said she could not live, but since life and death are in God's hand she astonished the doctors by living. However long the paralysis remains, we hope in God for complete healing. Having faced so many temptations from Satan, the Lord has trained us to fight him. We are not defeated in the battle; we are winners in Jesus Christ. Job's words are our testimony:

Wherefore do I take my flesh in my teeth, and put my life in my hand? Though he slay me, yet will I trust him: but I will maintain mine own ways before him (Job 13:14,15).

This book cannot be long enough to record all of the miracles and the salvation of God that we have beheld. The great God has divinely protected us from many accidents and dangers. His Word declares: *Let the redeemed say so!* Blessed be Jesus who enables us to praise Him.

Tekle's daughter Mehret and her daughter

Tekle with grandchildren

Granddaughter!

CHAPTER ELEVEN

FROM THE BEGINNING

By TEKLE

Through heart hunger and the earnest prayers of the Ethiopians a widespread outpouring of the Holy Ghost began in Ethiopia four years before Missionaries of the United Pentecostal Church came. By God's grace, I led blessed Holy Spirit revivals in many different areas and conducted night fellowship meetings in several places in Addis Ababa for three years before the Lord commanded me to go to Awassa, Sidamo, in 1969. On a visit to believers in Addis later that year I read in an American bulletin about the arrival of the Kenneth Wendells and we met by the will of God. I received the revelation of baptism in the name of Jesus, and the oneness of the Godhead through a tract Sister Wendell sent me, and I obeyed the Word.

God sent great revival in Awassa and the whole Sidamo region before I knew the whole truth, and with the truth, the flame of blessing leaped higher and spread farther-- over ten thousand souls baptized.

My witness of the baptism in Jesus Name revelation to church members I formerly worked with brought strong opposition. Trying to protect their members from this doctrine they didn't understand and labelled error, the leaders spoke to the people with false prophecies, imaginary visions, and dreams. At a night fellowship in Ato Tekleab's house, the leaders of the Full Gospel came at midnight and Brother Fantahun spoke in tongues for half an hour and in his supposed interpretation said in part, "Woe unto you who sow tares. I will come upon you and cut you off." In another phony interpretation, one said, "I am a God of love, not of disturbance. Keep your hearts, O my children; this spirit is not for you."

After prophesying out of their own hearts, they left. I recognized Fantahun is possessed of an evil spirit we did not know how to cast out. A few days later, as he preached at the Philadelphia mission in Awassa, he fell like a tree at the pulpit and wallowed, foaming at the mouth. We prayed and wept for him with fasting, but God did not deliver. He couldn't stay in the house; his family put his bed on the veranda. He lay there in painful suffering for three years before he died.

A spate of lying prophecies and schemes began. They distributed cassette tapes of so-called prophecies declaring "Tekle is dead" which caused utter confusion when the people saw me alive and well.

In Jimma, they told one of their members to be baptized by Brother Debena and come back screaming that she is demon possessed. They had the tape recorder ready to record her answer when they demanded, "Speak in Jesus Name. When did Satan enter into you?"

"When I went to the Apostolic Church to be baptized

in the name of Jesus. Reverend Debena baptized me and he is possessed by four demons."

Without shame, they took the cassette everywhere and played it for all who would listen until some began to realize the girl had lost her mind. Because of her lies the real Satan took possession of her and she became insane. Then they tried in vain to cast the devil out in the name of Jesus. It is amazing they didn't wonder if she became demon possessed by baptism in the name of Jesus, by whose name could they cast the devil out? By obeying her elders the poor girl surrendered to Satan and mocked the Name of the Holy God.

It happened according to the words of Isaiah quoted in John 12:38,40: *who hath believed our report? and to whom is the arm of the Lord revealed?...He hath blinded their eyes, and hardened their heart; that they should not with their eyes, nor understand with their heart, and be converted, and I should heal them.*

Brother Wendell had opened a church for the lepers in the French Legation. The nobility and others we had won usually gathered at the homes of Mama Solomie and Sister Sophia Asfaw for services. One Sunday (unfortunately on a clean-up day) some of them came in their Mercedes to Brother Wendells' service. With true humility they endured the stench and helped with the cleaning in spite of squeamish stomachs, but decided they should not bring a new soul to that place of smells and filth.

Finally, Brother Wendell began to understand the problem and rented a house of prayer for healthy people, first near the prison and later close to Mitchell Cotts. Brothers Amare, Solomon and Teshome came as fruit from that time and received assignments for the ministry. At this point the government forced the Wendells to leave the country; he closed the house and bought a piece of land at Gofa for a church and gave it to Brother Amare. With the difficulties in building a church, it became a school instead, and the fellowship met at Mama Worke's and Mama Solomie's.

Division came, Amare leading one group who worshiped in Mama Worke's house and me the others who met at Mama Awetash's house. More misunderstanding split Amare's group, and he transferred his work to Merkato. Persecution became stronger and the Kebele took the school which left them with no place to gather for worship. By the blessing of God, the prayer house I led grew in unity and power.

At a time when the government determinedly closed other denominations, Jesus told me to ask for land for a church building in the Gofa area. It looked impossible, but wonder of wonders, God moved on the communist government to give us an acre and a half of land. Building the church would take time, so we rented a house for worship at Saris. The Derg proclaimed, "No house fellowships; if people disobey this mandate, we will confiscate the house and close the meetings." They found us meeting in Saris and carried out their threats.

We had plans and needed to build big churches for the large congregations in both Wollayta and Chole, but before beginning that work, the brethren built a residence for my family on our land. Though we crowded in like sardines in a can, it became our meeting place until we could construct the new church.

By an incredible series of miracles and many dedicated helping hands, a creditable building went up.

Brother T.F. Tenney assisted by Brothers John Harris and E.L Freeman dedicated it for the glory of God. In a very short time it became as inadequate as our small house. We finally broke out a section of the wall and erected make-shift canvas sheets to partially cover the overflow, many times larger than those in the church.

Tekle and Erkenesh having lunch with
Brother Scism in their home

Country Churches

CHAPTER TWELVE

PROVEN FAITHFUL

By Dawit Iya

"Let me tell you how this salvation has proven true and powerful in Ado Shakso district." says Brother Dawit Iya and his faithful helper Addisu Barrso.

The Evangelical church reigned in this area for many years. We had our first service on Christmas day in 1986 in Utula, and from the beginning God smiled on us. Some of the people intrigued with a new name *The Apostolic Church* came out of curiosity, but they received the Holy Ghost. Most of the people hearing of this first became afraid of us, and soon, full of hatred, determined to chase this new religion out of their district.

A man in our village had an incorrigible son and determined for his good to take him to another village far away. Before a week passed the son died and the man returned home almost crazy with grief. We cast the demons out of him, which the Evangelical church had no power to do, and then like a flood, the hungry-hearted people came to us; many received healing.

The church without power used the scriptures to fight against us, referring to Matthew 24:24: *For there shall arise false Christ, and false prophets, and shall shew great signs and wonders; insomuch that, it were possible,they shall deceive the very elect.*

They declared our rejoicing and singing in the congregation came through demon possession quoting 2 Peter 2:13: *..count it pleasure to riot in the daytime...*But Jesus in respect to His name defended us. The more they spoke against us the more the people came to us.

While Brother Addisu and I preached in other places, they launched another plan and arrested scores of our saints and put them in prison. They threatened them: "If you will deny the Apostolic faith and return to your traditional church, we will release you; otherwise, we will arrest every one of this church."

All the brothers and sisters said, "We would rather die than leave our faith."

Then the Kebele leaders offered a compromise. "If you will not leave your faith, then you must not assemble together. Every man can pray in his own house with his wife. If you refuse this and meet together to pray, we will drive you out of town."

We took the preachers to a high mountain and met together in a dense forest to decide how to react to this ultimatum. I said to them, "A man can die of malaria or tuberculosis or some other disease, but if Jesus allows us to die, we would rather die for the sake of the Gospel. We have had enough of this earthly life and have chosen the kingdom of heaven hence we will meet on mountains and hills and shout for the victory; we refuse to be silent."

The people responded with all their hearts and said,

"The fellowship of the Apostolic church will assemble together until they eliminate us. As long as we live, we will be faithful."

When we met together in service that night I said, "Let us continue to worship boldly!"

The church responded with willingness and full joy and shouted "Amen!"

Our program continued with mighty rejoicing and clapping of hands as the Israelites going out to battle. Many people received healing and we cast eight demons out of a man who had suffered for a long time.

On hearing the sounds of our service, the leaders of the town snarled, "Do these people think they have freedom?" The next day they started arresting the believers again saying, "Didn't we command you not to assemble again? Who gave you permission to hold meetings? Now, we will put all of you in prison."

Abruptly, the Kebele leaders received orders from the District office conscripting them to close their offices and come help build houses for the peasants resettlement program. Though unhappy about it they had to go, so they released the prisoners. As we gathered that night, singing joyful songs with all our might they came and said, "We have to go build dwellings for the farmers, but we will arrest you when we come back."

Brother Dawit said, "Go ahead; we will sing until you return." They left in anger.

When they returned after more than a month away and found the church had multiplied in their absence they furiously began to round us up again. Before they could do much, news came from the inspectors that they had built so badly they must return and dismantle the building they erected and build a new one in its place. This hall, big enough to house ten peasant associations took some time to tear down and rebuild. They finally returned full of wrath ready to take vengeance on us, but a letter came from our headquarters in Addis Ababa saying the church has been registered and is no longer illegal. Our prosecutors stood dumbfounded when we showed them the letter. They seemed disappointed about being robbed of their prey, but thanks to Jesus, the giver of light, who did not allow their darkness to put out our light.

Then the Evangelical preachers intensified their preaching against us. They told the people, "These peoples' false doctrine came from overseas. Do not greet them, because they are possessed by a demon who came out of the dust. Run from them every time you see one. "

For a time, the people believed them and when we tried to witness, they would answer, "We have our church and our pastor." From the oldest to the youngest they avoided us. But we fasted and prayed, seeking God earnestly; He wrought miracles that opened doors.

A ten-year old member of a junior choir became acutely ill and when the prayers of church leaders availed nothing his family set out for the hospital some distance away. On the way they met a member of our church who said, "Why don't you go to this prayer meeting and let the Apostolics pray for him?"

Brother Abraham Dube, in charge of the meeting asked the family , "Are you religious?"

"We belong to the Evangelical church and our elders have prayed for the lad many times, but he is not healed. Eight members of our family have died with this disease that starts with a stomach ache. Please pray for him that he will live."

The preacher cast a demon out of the boy and he received total healing. The family returned home and continued in their traditional church and the boy became sick again. When the elders of the church prayed three days and nothing happened, his family said, "Let us take him to the Apostolic church before it is too late."

They brought him to me at Bufer and after prayer, healing came immediately. He ate food and regained strength, then his family asked that he stay with us so he can live.

In 1990, Lidya Ware, Isayas Barsso, and Genet Russie helped me pray for a man seventy-five years old who had been insane for many years. He continually threatened his family and wanted to slaughter them. When their books did not help, they finally called for us. The Lord healed him by our prayers; he and his whole family believed and began to work for the Lord. The people in the surrounding area then declared we have a great salvation.

A member of the Evangelical church named Racha Halake became very sick in 1991 and lost his mind. His church elders prayed for him until he said one day, "I will die in nine days." They became disgusted and abandoned him. His family had heard that the Apostolics heal insane people so they brought him to me with his bruised hands and feet tightly bound. I said, "Loose him." He became normal immediately when we prayed and the following day received complete healing. He arose and declared, "Brethren, I was dead, but now I am alive, Praise Jesus!" He could hardly stop glorifying God. He and his whole family believed and came to the Apostolic church.

Bullala Sersa, 120 years old became ill and told his

family, "I will be dead in three days." His oldest son came to me and begged me to go pray for him. He said, "The disease that will kill my father is Satan. Even if he lives a few more days, he will die with the devil in him. Whether he lives or dies, I want to bury my father's body clean; please pray for him."

I went home with him and told the family, "You simply believe and the old man will be healed." I prayed for him at 7:00 P.M.. The next morning he got up and said, "I was dead, but now I am free from death. I thank Jesus." Now, he is in the church.

At the same time a 115 year old man who had been seriously ill for six years sent a messenger to call us. When we found him he said, "I believe in the way of truth, but this disease burns me like a fire. I am not able to sit, sleep, or stand; I prefer death to this torment, but if you can heal me by the power of prayer I will obey whatever you require of me. If you say separate yourself from your family or your wealth so that I can be healed, I will do it with my whole heart." We prayed and complete healing came.

The people who knew this man heard about his healing and said, "Those Apostolics not only heal the sick and cast out demons, but now they have modified old age. God is really with them. If you want salvation, go to them!"

On the January 25, 1993 believers both old and young came to Utulu to start the church. Everyone forgot positions or honor and we all worked together for the glory of God. It seemed most of the population came to hear our songs and sermons and to see the work of the church done between Monday and Sunday that week. This annoyed the Evangelical church and some of them shouted at us angrily and threatened to burn the house and kill us. The outsiders said, "Not even God would destroy such a magnificent house!" They praised the Lord and blessed us. Everyone testified they had never seen such a marvelous work done by the power of God in such a short time.

We had difficulties constructing the church due to a scarcity of water in that place and the winter weather. The people worried about their cattle since all the ponds had dried up. We cried to the Lord for help and He sent abundant rains filling the ponds again, and the work prospered. Blessed be our God who always makes a way for His children!

General Board at Wara Crusade. Dawitt, lower center

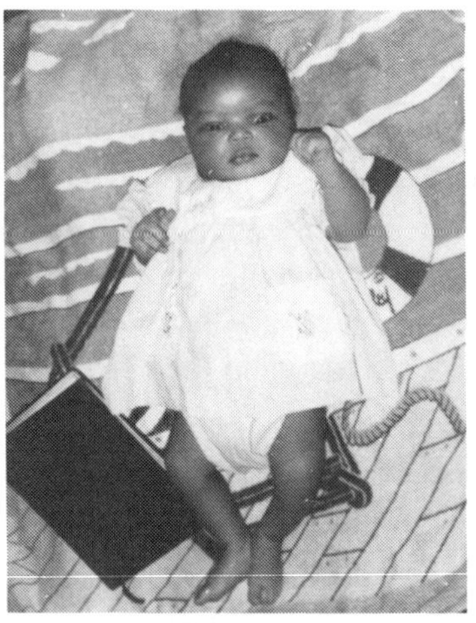

Granddaughter Haimonot

Dedicating church at Ziway

Ayele (r) next to General Jagama, Head of
the Army under Haile Selassie. His life
spared through church's prayers. Ayele's
parents, foreground.

74

CHAPTER THIRTEEN

GROWTH IN JEMJEM

The work of God began when a lad of ten received the Holy Ghost, and from 1980 the Spirit has fallen like rain upon the Guji tribes. God revealed the truth to Godana, a Lutheran pastor at Murri, by the young student. He and two other brothers went to Alleta Wondo to be baptized in Jesus name and returned to teach his flock the truth. When three hundred people got baptized in Jesus name on September 10, 1981 the Lutheran church reacted with wholesale persecution against all who obeyed the Word, taking men and women to jail.

After I went to Anaheim, California, USA for the General Conference of the UPCI, my wife Erkenesh, according to plans made before I left, went to Jemjem with Sister Menbere and Brother Dejene to teach the new converts. The amazing move in Jemjem probably came about as a result of Erkenesh's prayer. She felt heavily burdened for this area for a long time. In Borre, the travellers asked a policeman about a certain street and he immediately arrested them and put them in jail. The police took away their suitcases, food, and blankets; they suffered from hunger, from cold, and from insects that crawled out of the dirt floor to torment them. (Ethiopian prisons do not feed prisoners).

No one knew what had happened for some time. Feeling deep concern, I phoned my home repeatedly from America but could learn nothing. Men in charge of the prison came in the cell holding Erkenesh, Sister Membere, and other women, locked the door behind them, and announced their evil intentions. Erkenesh quietly bound them in the name of Jesus and the men began to tremble so violently they struggled to get the door unlocked so they could leave. Later, they put the women on the porch and dared one another to molest them, but every one who started up the steps began to shake so hard they practically fell down the steps to get away.

Erkenesh overheard the officials say, "Those Pentes have killed so many; we have brought them to jail." Her heart sank. The people had not been saved long and she wondered if the devil had pulled them away so quickly. A spate of inter-tribal fighting and outlaw thievery caused much trouble at this time and some of these culprits had been arrested. Erkenesh watched for a chance to learn more and asked the wounded people, "What church do you belong to?" When they answered "Evangelical," she felt relieved.

About this time Brother Godana learned the truth and notified our family in Addis. When I got the news and told Brother Freeman about Erkenesh's cruel situation, he asked if I wanted to return home at once and not wait for the conference. I answered, "No, we will just pray earnestly for her deliverance. If I could talk to her, I feel sure she would say, 'Do what you went to America to do, but PRAY!'"

The prison officials notified the police headquarters

in Addis Ababa that I had fled to America, and they arrested Erkenesh because they caught her trying to flee to Kenya. They made plans to confiscate the headquarters church in Addis, but our neighbor General Tadesse Ferede, a senior government official knew that I travelled legally, so he blocked them. He then ordered Erkenesh released from the inhuman torture of the prison.

The great revival in the area where Brother Godana pastored did not touch the district secretary of the peasant Association, Ato Tadesse Duko. Because Godana revealed the imprisonment of Erkenesh, Duko angrily made plans to arrest him and take him to the same jail. Before he could carry out his plans against Godana, he participated in a horse race. His horse took a bad fall with him, and his skull burst open and his brains fell out causing instant death.

The Murri church has gone through many hardships. Though their church burned two times, they became the first church to reach a membership of one thousand members in Jemjem. Addo Wacho came with a new rifle and boasted he would put one bullet in the twice rebuilt church to set it afire. But an angel of God put unseen fire on his body and no one could come near him because of the heat. He suffered horribly for five days before he died screaming continually, "The God of the Apostolic church is burning me to death!" Even after death, water poured over the body could not cool it, a blanket dipped in water sent up clouds of steam and they could only bury him after they wound his body with tree limbs and leaves.

People saw how mightily the hand of God moved in answer to our prayers in Jesus name and came from everywhere to receive healing and deliverance from all their diseases and demon possession.. When we sang the demons screamed and came out of the possessed. The ones touched by God went home and witnessed from village to village. The Gospel reached many provinces in a short time.

When news of this happening went out, many heathen came to repentance. In Murri Mulato, all the members of fifteen Evangelical churches came to repentance and we baptized them in the Malawe River in 1992. The Gospel extended to the Adolla and Borre districts where many heathen and nominal church members found salvation. The administrators of both districts became angry and began persecutions in earnest.

In Borre, the district secretary Ato Alemseged Berhe made severe difficulties for the Gospel work until we prayed earnestly for deliverance. Then officials found he had embezzled government money and arrested him. He hanged himself with his belt in prison, and the church had rest.

When the Administrator of Adolla returned from burning ten of our churches he found one of his sons dead; shortly afterward a second son died. He realized God's hand had touched him heavily and declared, "I will never touch these people again." Thus we received liberty to assemble freely and expand the Gospel throughout the region.

A group of people later met in Adolla to devise a method to eliminate the Apostolic churches, and a terrible thunder storm struck the house and killed all of them.

The chief register, our worst opponent in Borre town, had a seriously ill daughter. Spending all his money he took her to different hospitals, to wizards, and holy water fountains; but the girl grew worse. Finally, as the last hope, with humble apologies and a contrite heart, he came to the people he had tried to kill. After prayer his daughter received instant healing, and though lame before, she jumped up and walked home.

A rich man named Tesfaye Yilma who lived in Borre had an insane son who would not stay in the house but wandered in the jungle shouting and babbling day and night. Some of the saints told his father, "If you will take your son to the Apostolic church he will be restored to normal."

The father didn't pay much attention at first for he had taken the boy many places for five years trying to find help. Besides the boy could run as fast as a car travels, and if they caught him they couldn't hold him. One day someone caught him and his father bound him with chains and brought him to the church. When the leaders prayed for him, Jesus healed him instantly. Now Tesfaye supports the church, and since he is a famous man, the people who oppose us must be quiet.

The good Word spread to Aroresa; twenty-two churches sent for Brother Godana to baptize them. Because of this, enemies of the truth burned their church buildings. The saints gathered with humility and prayed on the ashes. Because of their sweet spirit and long-suffering, God did many remarkable miracles and their numbers increased. A group of people from different denominations came to challenge us and the Spirit caused them to surrender to the Gospel.

Denominational leaders forbade their members to greet or even speak to the Apostolics. They couldn't separate them, for they live in the same place and many are blood relations. Our people feel the burden to witness to everyone and believe they can win at least one soul a week. Moslems came repenting and got baptized and wizards brought their instruments of sorcery and burned them so they could follow the Lord. When the flow of new believers increased more than they could handle, the preachers asked Brother Godana to come to Gura Wotano to teach the people. Immediately severe persecution broke out; they baptized ninety-nine people at night and left. The new saints stood firm, even though the enemy burned their homes.

The worst persecution came in 1986-87. Ato Mamo Bitaye, the district administrator, burned eight churches in one day. He brought his militia, surrounded Brother Wako's church and fired many rounds of bullets while the saints inside bowed before the Lord and prayed. It made the militia angry when they burst inside and found the people all alive so they beat them unmercifully. The administrator led his men away feeling happy over their unmerciful deeds. On the way home someone invited them for a feast on a fat goat. Somehow, the fat meat did not set well with the administrator; his stomach swelled until it almost burst and he died. Many believers escaped injury since this cruel man passed away, for he planned to completely do away with the Apostolic church.

In the locality of Awaye, the husband and family of an insane woman got tired of trying to keep her chained up and abandoned her. One day the villagers told him, "A healing religion has come to our district and they heal people like your wife. Why don't you take her?"

He answered, "I am fed up with healers; I have tried many of them and they all failed, maybe I will try it."

He took her and by prayer in the name of Jesus, the devils came out and she immediately received the Holy Ghost. Through this all of her family followed the Lord and a church has been established in their village where miracles happen in every service. The deaf hear, the dumb speak, and many near to death with swollen abdomens or other serious ailments are carried in on stretchers and leave leaping and rejoicing.

Bayu Dukale, a member of the Lutheran church, came to challenge the church in a conference. Before he could ask the questions the Gospel preached by different ministers broke his heart and brought him to his knees. After his baptism in the Name of Jesus he received the Holy Ghost and returned to witness to the fifty churches in his area. Many of them received the message gladly; 1,035 experienced baptizm in the river in one day. Today, Brother Bayu pastors more than three thousand souls.

Genale Arere, a leader of fifty-two churches, came to us lately. Having received and obeyed the truth, he returned to his province using wisdom to convince the churches to follow the Word of God. We have received a message now that all understand and a large baptismal service will be held soon.

A minister of the Evangelical Church, Ayele Arere walked two days from Hagre Mariam determined to prove the Apostolic doctrine wrong. The Spirit of the Lord defeated him and with a broken heart he obeyed the Lord. He returned home and now is leading a great revival.

The Gospel spreads swiftly with power and wonder works. In nine years 38,261 souls have been baptized in Jemjem. If the Lord continues to work at this rate, we believe the rest of the population will come to the true Gospel shortly. We trust the current 120 churches will be multiplied many fold.

Man marked with circle 1 came to kill
Tekle; now a might preacher of the Gospel

Church too small

CHAPTER FOURTEEN

BORENA REVIVAL

The revival in Borena, Liban province, began in a surprising manner. In 1980 more than six hundred members of the Lutheran Church decided to study their Bibles in-depth on the Apostles doctrine and manner of working with a determination to follow their example. After three years of study, prayer, and intercession, they heard of the Apostolic Church. Encouraged by the contact, Tesfaye Gelesaw, a government school teacher, transferred to Negelle, Borena for closer contact with the leaders. Through his ministry Brother Abraham and several other leaders had a revelation of the mystery of truth and wanted to be baptized in Jesus Name.

Since Tesfaye came from Wollayta, he took them by car a two-day journey to Brother Dawit in Wollayta for baptism. Brother Dawit promised to come to Borena later to baptize others who desired to follow the Lord. When they arrived to keep that appointment water could not be found. Finally, they baptized six hundred people in a well dug by the Evangelical Church.

A lady missionary from Europe who lived long in the

area became so upset over the Holy Ghost falling in their Lutheran schools, hospitals, and churches she bribed the district administrator, Ato Liben, to force the former members to return to the church. While the first Apostolic conference convened with about a thousand people present, Liben sent the militia to surround them.

He started a false rumor that we had armed the people and fled to a neighboring country. The only arms the believers had in their hands was the Word of God. Liben's men separated the men from the women, stripped off all their clothes, and tortured them cruelly. He then offered them papers, "If you will sign this form promising to return to the Lutheran Church, we will stop the torture."

"We received nothing from the Lutheran Church but some used clothing and a little wheat," the people answered. "In the Apostolic Church we have received life and power. We would rather die than return."

God sent a cruel angel to kill the tormenters who carried out Liben's orders; their bodies swelled horribly. In intense pain they felt as if rats ran up and down in their veins for several days before they died. The missionary contracted a quick-acting leprosy-like disease and lost body parts one by one until she died. Liben failed with the communists and now is in big trouble, but the Gospel spreads like wild fire.

In September 1987, Brother Isayas went to witness in the Watts Buri locality. With mockery some of the people brought a twenty-six year old insane woman who had been bound for eighteen years and could no longer walk; "We have heard you Pentes can heal people. Let's see you heal this woman!"

Brother Isayas answered, "I cannot heal, but Jesus

who lives in me can heal her." By the time he finished giving a Bible lesson, numerous snakes appeared from nowhere and circled the woman. Nothing deterred, Brother Isayas rebuked them and commanded the demons to come out of the woman in Jesus Name. With a last cry of agony forty demons fled and the snakes disappeared. Then he said, "Stand up and walk in Jesus name!" The young woman jumped up and started walking--she is still healthy and normal, today.

Then the people said, "The Apostolic Church has a true healer God!"

On May 18, 1990, Brother Yosef was forced to attend a local meeting, leaving his church without a pastor that day. A blind man came to his church seeking healing and not finding Yosef went to the meeting looking for him. The people present looked at Yosef and at the blind man and began to mock, "How can this foolish blind man think he will be healed in a Pente church. Ha ha!." Everyone's tongue started wagging and Yosef was glad to get away when the meeting finally ended.

He took the man to his church and prayed for him, "O Lord, your name is despised by the heathen. We are also despised. Now, Lord, for your holy name's sake will you look upon this blind man and restore his sight."

Nothing happened and the blind man went home. He wakened in the night and looked to the right and could see his surroundings, then looked left and saw everything clearly. With mounting excitement he woke up the whole family, "I can see! I can see!"

Skeptically, his father pointed out different objects. "What is this? What is that?" When he correctly identified everything his father indicated, he realized, "Truly, my son can see!"

When word went out about the miracle in the name of Jesus Christ, the people who mocked feared and the village elders said, "These Jesus only people are different and their God is different. If anyone touches them, death will follow him. Watch out for these people." These words ended persecution in that area and the church reaches out in every direction.

The culture of Borena and the Gospel are diametrically opposed; when a landlord dies, his son is his successor and must throw every child born to him for the next eight years to the hyenas. This is supposed to protect the rest of his children from the plague. Members of each tribe are under an obligation to kill a man from another tribe, otherwise they think Satan will attack them. When one took the initiative and killed a man from another tribe, war costing the lives of many people began and stopped only when the state intervened.

Since our church expands between the Guji and Borena tribes, the elders of each tribe, zealous of maintaining the old ways, became both annoyed and fearful. They feared Satan might be angry and kill them if they did not do something. Elders from five localities met together to discuss this critical matter. They realized they could not bring the people back to a heathen culture, so they decided to destroy the people who brought this religion to their area. On July 25, 1990 they made a resolution to kill forty Apostolic Church preachers. They invited them to come for a meeting with a pretense of good-will.

On the third day of a three-day prayer and fasting, the preachers made the day-long journey to the appointed place where the village elders had hidden guns and rods.

Because of fasting and the tedious journey the preachers trembled with weakness; though their appearance startled the elders they still said, "We demand that you forsake Jesus."

The brethren realized they had walked into a trap, but Jesus did not fail. A strong anointing came on them and they declared the Gospel to the elders, one by one. The elders angrily grabbed their guns and the preachers turned to flee. When the first man shot at them, the bullet exploded in the gun barrel. Five more men lifted their guns and tried to shoot, but none of the guns would fire. The preachers escaped. After walking some distance, feeling weary and weak, they lay down to rest on top of a hill. When a gazelle running from a monkey came and stood in their midst, they killed and cooked it. Strengthened by the meat, they easily made the rest of the journey in safety; however, the persecution did not slack.

The angel of the Lord smote the family of the man who led this conspiracy and attempted to kill the forty preachers. As his wife and children hung between death and life, he went to a wizard for help. The wizard told him, "Your family has been smitten by God, and if you don't apologize to the people you have persecuted and tried to kill, your family will die."

The wizard's words frightened him very much and he could not believe the brethren would trust and accept him, but the Lord gave him courage. He got on his horse and galloped to see Brother Yoseph and the other brethren. Falling at their feet with humble apologies he begged them to please go home with him and pray for his family. Without suspicion or doubt, several of the preachers went with him to his home and prayed, and the Lord instantly healed all of them. In gratitude the man gave his farm for the construction of a church.

A rude young communist named Charo Bleda boasted to Brother Addisu, "I will destroy the church in Shakiso town."

Brother Addisu replied, "Those who destroy the house of God will be destroyed by God."

Charo went crazy that very night. His parents tied him with a rope and brought him to Brother Addisu for prayer, God delivered him and now he lives in the fear of God.

In Harkness vicinity of Shakiso Province, a young man named Yohannes Lalfa suffered severely from leprosy. His family brought him to the Apostolic Church for prayer, and the ministry cast the devil out of him. The same night healthy skin replaced his ugly diseased skin, and he enjoyed perfect healing. Out of gratitude, his family started a fellowship in their house which quickly expanded to a large church, and the name of Jesus is glorified in that village.

Village church

CHAPTER FIFTEEN

SIDAMO

"Go to Awassa!" The Lord Jesus gave Tekle this direct call and he obeyed on January 28, 1968 and started a church. He reached out to Titira and Aleta Wondo and the churches grew rapidly, especially Titira because of big miracles done by the name of Jesus. Soon six thousand people overflowed the church pastored by Erkenesh's brother, Tamiur and Brother Zerihun. The Lord directed Tekle to space the churches five kilometers apart. Instead of crowding all the saints in one church, let the people travelling long distances build churches in their own village and witness to their neighbors to fill it. The two pastors would not cooperate with Tekle's instruction because they loved money.

The Lord aimed at spreading the revival quickly, and though the pastors did not support Tekle's directions, the people did. In a short time thirty churches sprang up, and before long they increased to sixty churches. When Tamiur saw this he became an enemy and accused Tekle as a CIA agent to the government. Zerihun, motivated by greed conspired with Ato Hailu, the presbyter of Sidamo Section and negotiated with the Evangelical Church to sell them our churches. When Tekle realized what was happening, he called the pastors and saints together and led by the Spirit of God, they rejected the trio as leaders.

Ato Hailu returned to the Evangelical Church and wrote false reports hoping to replace the money he lost from the government. The three men determined by any means, including murder, to spoil Tekle's name and the name of the church by giving slanderous reports to the communist cadres.

A carbon copy of a letter written by Ato Hailu fell into our hands that read as follows:

Our prosecutors didn't succeed, the God who protected us has fought for us. A battle took place between the devils who stood for them and the angels who stood for us--ours won, and we go on with victory. Two have died and one is suffering on the earth.

The Evangelicals in Yirgalem bought the regional secretary of the Workers Party of Ethiopia with a lot of money to put an end to the churches from Aleta, Dalle District, Shebedino, Bensa, Arerssa, Dilla, to Awassa and surrounding districts. When he received the money he boasted, "I will destroy them in one day, don't worry."

Fortunately Tekle suspected what would happen and before the district administrators had time to act on the secret messages and begin destroying the churches he went to the Commissioner for security of the party and showed him the letter about the bribed man. He made an application for protection of the churches telling the number of people and churches in every district. The size of the work shocked the Commissioner and he called all of the administrators and changed his word, "Don't touch these people, since the case is very risky."

Because the dead lived again, the blind received sight, and the sick found deliverance from all manner of diseases by the power in the name of Jesus, the church being strengthened gave birth to churches until the enemies of the Gospel trembled in fear.

The daughter of the minister in Leku town Shebedino died. The place had only one graveyard belonging to the Orthodox Church. The preacher asked permission to bury his daughter there and they refused. The body lay at home for two days and on the third day, the police forced the church to allow the burial. The people rioted and tried to kill the believers. When the police left, the priests agitated the people to beat our people unmercifully and to destroy their property.

Though robbed and naked the saints encouraged themselves with prayer and witnessing. When they prayed for a well-known man of the town who had been sick for many years the Lord raised him up; this turned the heart of the townspeople toward the church again. In a short time eleven Evangelical churches came repenting and were baptized in the name of Jesus. Within a few months the Lord helped the ministers to found forty-seven churches in Shebedino. The government began to respect this sizeable segment of the population and gave them cemeteries in every town. With the lies of the denominations against them proven false, the churches now have rest and are encircled with glory and praise.

When someone witnessed to Nejo, a wealthy nominal church member and saloon keeper, he accepted the whole Gospel, closed the bar, and obeyed God's call to step out full time in the ministry. He began by witnessing at the nearby Evangelical church and the young people followed him at once, the adults came later, except for the elders who had two wives. All of them received the Holy Ghost and got baptized in the name of Jesus.

Alarmed, leaders of his old church came from Addis Ababa and Awassa with flattery to entice him and his converts to return, but they did not succeed. He built a beautiful church on his farm and before long this church had started seven branch works and is wealthy in healings and miracles.

In a conference June 28 at his gate the Lord healed many people before the ministry had a chance to lay hands on them. This convinced observers from the Evangelical Church and the heathen of the power of the Gospel. Village leaders who supported the work defeated the arguments of denominational critics who tried to hinder the conference.

Brother Nejo's wife suffered from acute urethral disease and went to Tikur Anbess hospital for surgery. The doctor made a serious mistake and left her unable to control her urine. A second operation made matters worse and the doctors told her nothing could be done to help her. Prayer with anointing oil in the name of Jesus stopped the pain and restored her to normal. This unexpected miracle astounded the community who responded by gathering up many patients suffering from a wide variety of diseases and bringing them to the church for prayer. All of them received complete healing.

Molla Bedamo's wife, Tutu lived naked and foolishly insane, before believing prayer delivered her. Her healing brought her husband to full salvation, and soon afterward, he quit his job and started a church in his hotel in Leku, and began to witness to everyone who would listen. He became a man of amazing faith, outstanding healings;

people raised from the dead became a regular feature of his ministry long before time for his ordination.

A man who saw his sick children made whole by Brother Molla's prayer gave him land to build a bigger church and the miracles continued. Thirteen Evangelical churches became converted under his teaching, so within three months he represented fourteen churches which expanded rapidly. He previously did a good work as a member of the Sudan Inland Mission, and in the truth, God gave him immense favor with all the Apostolic Churches. At a minister's conference in his district, the preachers chose Brother Molla for their presbyter. Tremendous growth in the whole area followed this move.

Our oldest Apostolic Church in Awassa, begun by Brother Tekle, still has many of the original members who bravely tasted the indignity of arrest and endured torture serving God firmly in every circumstance. Before the formal organization of the church, they sacrificed to keep the ministry alive by forming Mother and Father Auxiliaries to feed them.

During the pastorate of an aged preacher named Hailu Fantaw we obtained 16,500 square yards of land for a church. With amazing strength Hailu dug a well, planted trees and built a church about 30x50. He felt deeply grieved over the closing of the church by the Derg, but kept the church body alive by ministering from house to house in those perilous times. Even though the Cadres threatened to confiscate any home used for prayer, faithful followers of the Lord offered to sacrifice their homes by allowing the saints to gather in them for worship.

When Brother Ashenafi became pastor with the support of an attorney and the ministry of Town

Development, he laid a claim against the city stating that the church is the legal property of the Apostolic church and should be restored to the believers. They won the case in court; the decision standing even against an appeal from the city council of Awassa. Those men tried in vain to kill Ashenafi, but we regained possession of our church in 1990.

The recording angel has written the names of godly men who contributed to the widespread of the Gospel in Sidamo, the province where the greatest Jesus Name revival ever known is happening. Names that sound strange to American ears, but are well-known to our sovereign God; Legesse Lankamo, Samuel Godadmo, Worku Berede, Tadesse Doyamo, Dawitt Iya, Eyob Buie, Gebresillassie Mantesso, Paulos Wajego and Mekuria Merso. These men endured hardships and prison for the name of Jesus, but tasted His strength and rejoiced in His mercy through it all.

When physical difficulties slackened, they faced a more subtle temptation as other churches tried to buy their services; however, with good understanding of the wiles of the enemy and the Word, they lifted high the banner of truth and remained faithful. Most of them still serve as leaders today.

Because Sidamo is a densely populated area, God led Tekle and his board to lay down strict rules for establishing churches. If any believers had to walk more than a half hour to get to church, a branch work must be opened. Some of the pastors did not like this rule at first, (fearing to lose members and tithes) but it has provided a rapidly advancing outreach. The pastors would open branch churches half an hour's walk away on either side and assign capable assistants to take charge, giving them half of the tithes for the first year until they had proven themselves. With the people's respect for the ministry and spiritual authority, no one would consider trying to change churches. This eliminated arguments about boundaries and maintained the evangelistic thrust. Each pastor is required to report his progress in fulfilling this plan.

Acting on reports from informers from the Evangelical and Philadelphia churches, Mekonnen Fara, administrator of Aroressa gave cruel orders to beat the saints of the Apostolic Church and rob them of their property. The enemies of the church went from farm to farm to abuse the believers, destroy their property, and slaughter their goats for private feasts.

Hailu Fantaw and Samuel Jejerso, carrying instructions from the Regional Administrator, went to try solve the problem. Though Mekonnen realized he had acted illegally, he still gave them many hassles until the Lord helped the brothers settle the case. As more and more people left the traditional powerless churches and streamed to the Apostolic church, they are no longer victimized--their size instills fear in the hearts of ungodly leaders.

Dawit, the leader of the Hagerselam sub-section cannot read and write, but his children read to him and he has memorized so much of the Bible and understands its mysteries so well, no one realizes the lack. God has decorated him with administrative wisdom, divine favor, and glory. Everyone he prays for is healed, whether blind, deaf, or diseased. One blind man healed by Dawit's prayer has learned to read and is now a pastor with an unusual blessing on his ministry. Dawit enjoys unusual favor from government authorities by his gift for stopping problems before they begin--with his discerning reports to them, they can nip trouble in the bud. Churches in his area are growing.

A noted wizard in Hagerselam deceived people for twenty-one years. They came from different places to bow before him and he exploited the fifty to a hundred people who came to consult him daily. Some days he slaughtered twenty cows going through his weird rituals. One day his gods rejected him, refused his sacrifices, and several of his wives and children died suddenly, leaving him with one wife and a daughter. In desperation he went to a more famous wizard seeking mercy from his gods. The man told him, "It would be good for you to believe in only one God."

Immediately, he went to a nearby Apostolic Church and pled with the pastor, "Please tell me about faith in one God."

The pastor answered from the Word of God; the beautiful story of Jesus the Savior, who gave His life to redeem sinners, and now commands everyone to be baptized in His name. The ex-wizard believed and after his baptism according to Acts 2:38, the preacher went home with him to pray for his wife and daughter who hung between life and death. Both of them received healing and his wife instantly got up to show customary hospitality to their visitor!

Since the wizard had been extremely popular, his conversion shook the whole community and the believers glorified the Lord. More than one hundred people have been baptized in the name of Jesus because the wizard and his family followed Jesus.

Paulos Wojogo did not read well, but he became a forceful witness after receiving a revelation of the truth and brought many trinitarian churches to righteousness. He lived in a dangerous place, the boundary of Arsi and Sidamo where people fought to the death over grazing land. Since Paulos brought the gospel that opened a door of peace, he is beloved of the Arsis.

The fighting and killing has gone on from one generation to another without mercy. Since there are now apostolics on both sides of the border who strive to live in peace, things are changing. In the last fighting many heathen died, but none of the saints. The government now understands that true salvation brings peace and gives every consideration to Paulos and the brethren who work with him.

In a recent meeting in Awassa of the Administrator with various church leaders, they demanded, "Block the Apostolics! They are taking all our people."

"Don't make that kind of request--let religion alone," he replied, "We don't try to stop the politicians from trying to get the people to support them. Besides who else can give the people release from chat, tobacco, marijuana, and alcohol that makes them prisoners in their own house? We need free people filled with peace and love, hence the Gospel must be preached on city squares, in the streets, and in houses. Do not bind your members. Give them liberty to go to the church of their choice. I want you to sign an agreement to this at once."

Many of the leaders felt unhappy with the adminstrator's ultimatum. They knew their work would go down while the truth flourished. Some chose to ignore the paper they signed and shot into the houses of people baptized in the name of Jesus. The new believers said, "You cannot force us to live a lie, we will obey truth at any cost."

Others said, "We built this building with our own hands and with our own money. Since all of us are leaving, why must we go without a building? Let us reject this preacher and find one who knows the truth to preach to us in our own church building." This has brought much confusion to their leaders.

At a meeting in Woyecho for Evangelists and Auxiliaries in October 1992, two denominational churches brought us food, saying, "We will help you feed your guests." They came pretending friendliness, but they had put malathine (poison) in the food. We had to take sixteen people who ate that food to the doctor with severe poisoning. One of our brothers testified. "Since we cannot identify the guilty ones, we will leave vengeance to God. We must be alert and not allow jealousy in our hearts, because jealousy is dangerous. That is why Satan killed Jesus and he will not pardon us who follow Jesus Christ."

Since the police know these people's plan to fight us, we always notify them about our conferences. Now, they send forces to encircle us with protection until the last service. The miracles that bring many to the Lord continue unabated.

Ato Bolka Lemasso of the Sidamo tribe served as a member of parliament under the reign of Haile Selasse; he entertained the King at the cultural center he built at his own expense in Midregenet, Shebedino Province. Even today he is highly respected and very popular. On August 26 he went from his home to the Evangelical Church. When he reached the gate, he suddenly became blind and lost his direction. When he tried to enter the gate, everything became black before him. He tried to look right and left and could only see the Leku Apostolic church quite far away. Since darkness covered his church, he turned away from the gate and walked toward the Apostolic church. When he reached its gate, he knelt and prayed and wanted to go home, but the darkness returned and Brother Jugsa's son took him by the hand and led him home.

At home, the Lord spoke to him to read the book of Acts, and when he opened the Bible his sight returned. As he read from the first chapter to the last, he understood the apostle's doctrine is true and encouraged his family to accept the truth.

Bolka has the problem of two wives and refused to be baptized with his first wife as the church leaders instructed him, but he never misses a service. His first wife has received the Holy Ghost, though is not yet baptized. The new church in Midregenet has 270 members and they rejoice knowing God can do the impossible.

Bozalech Borja led the Saint Mary's Fellowship of the Orthodox church and enjoyed honor and respect from all its members. After she became severely paralyzed in 1989, her family took her to many places of holy waters in search of healing to no avail. Finally they brought her to Leku Apostolic church, where God instantly healed her and she received the Holy Ghost when the pastor baptized her in Jesus name for remission of her sins.

When the Saint Mary's Association heard of her healing and conversion, they called her husband in and warned him, "We will cancel your membership and take your name out of the benevolent society unless you forbid your family to go to that Pente church. Also, when you die, you will not be buried."

"How can I lose a graveyard and have my name spoiled and cancelled from the association in the place where I have lived, respected by all the people for so long? he asked his wife. "This cannot be. So starting from today, none of my family is allowed to go to the mission church." From that time he began persecuting his wife and his children, but they held fast to the truth.

On September 15 he gave an ultimatum, "If you go to that church again, I will not allow you to ever enter this house...". Before he could finish his speech Satan threw him to the floor with paralyzed limbs and his words ended in a scream. When death seemed eminent, the Orthodox priest came and prayed as he sprinkled water on him, but he remained bound. They took him to other places for treatment in vain.

When the priests saw he is near death one said, "Your house is unclean because of the Pentes, we cannot come and pray for you after you die. You should go to your other daughter's home who is Orthodox and die there so we can pray for you better."

"I perceive you cannot help me; you are no benefit to me. How dare you tell me go out of my house before I die. I forbid you to ever come to my house again and don't bury me in your graveyard when I die. Use your prayers for yourself, but from this day on I am a member of the Apostolic Church."

He immediately sent for the leaders of the church; God healed him through their prayers and he now worships Jesus freely with his family.

Getu Melkamu, a teacher, had a nervous breakdown and became totally insane. His family took him to wizards and holy waters to no avail and finally committed him to the mental hospital in Addis Ababa. After seven years they brought him home and put him bound with chains in a locked room, but his yelling and screaming disturbed the whole neighborhood.

One day he broke the chains and escaped from the room and went berserk--he beat several people and injured others before the people could catch him and bind him again with chains. On January 30, 1988 they brought him to Leku Apostolic church and one prayer delivered him from Satan's power. He returned to work normal and well, and his testimony has converted many lost souls.

Burnt by hot metal rods, Senbaba Sewaku suffered from maggot-infested wounds that would not heal for many years. The odor from his infections kept everyone at a distance. He tried holy waters, local medicines, and hospitals. Nothing helped. Exhausted by suffering and treatment that didn't work, he made his last will and testament thinking death would claim him soon. Instead, someone took him to Leku Apostolic church for prayer. Within a week he not only received total healing for his body, but found full and free salvation for his soul. The church reaped another harvest of souls as a result of this miracle.

Her body bowed and trembling so she could not walk unaided, Kun Tsegaye endured possession by Satan for twenty-six years. The custodians of holy waters, wizards, magicians, and hospitals all pronounced her case hopeless. She lost her money and property and became a lonely derelict without hope. Her family heard that a demon possessed niece who had been in and out of jail for years had found deliverance at the Leku church, so they brought Kun. The prayer of faith cast out of her forty demons who left screaming. Then Kun, her trembling gone, stood straight, got baptized at once and received the Holy Ghost.

On September 30, 1988 four-year old Demelash Jigso choked on his food and died at ten A.M. and word of his death spread through the village. When prayers touched heaven he came back to life two hours later and the Lord sang this song through him; "Yesus breho Nazerethun ho reyetnore belite hare fushinoho." Translated it means, "Jesus is peace to the burdened and life for those who taste death."

A powerful demon possessed Merekie Samego and though his family travelled far and wide, they could find no help for him. After prayer at the Leku church the demon abandoned him and he followed the Lord in baptism and received the Holy Ghost. With his life changed, his whole family and many friends became converted. Because of this two new churches have been opened at Dilla Olkana and Allawo; each enjoys great revival and have more than two hundred souls.

The wife of Zeneke Bolka stepped out of her house at 9:00 P.M. in 1989 and Satan, in the form of a man, attacked her and threw her at the door and ran away. She screamed, "The man has killed me. Help! Help!" Her husband grabbed a knife and chased the man-like figure for an hour; then as he disappeared in thin air, he realized, "This is not a man; it is a demon."

When he returned home, he found his wife, with her mind confused and her right wrist broken, still lying on the ground. His neighbors helped him carry her to Leku church, and with prayer her wrist instantly became whole and the demon departed. She obeyed Acts 2:38 and her husband followed her example. Now, many more souls have found the Lord through this remarkable deliverance.

Bekele Woldemeskel, a faithful deacon in the Orthodox church had a yearly feast honoring Gabriel, usually killing ten oxen to feed the people who came. One day when he returned from celebrating the ark of Gabriel, a rampaging demon entered him and he went wild. He burned his house down and killed his cattle, then his body began to swell horribly. His family tied him on a bed and brought him to

Fura Apostolic church for prayer. Jesus touched him, the swelling disappeared and the demon screaming left him.. Twenty people followed him through the waters of baptism in the name of Jesus and all of them received the glorious Holy Ghost with the evidence of speaking in other tongues.

Like the lady in the Bible, Elizabeth Waire had an issue of blood for twelve years and wandered many places seeking relief and found none. The odor of her sickness kept everyone at a distance. Finally she went to the Apostolic church in Hagereselam and received healing through prayer. She obeyed the Gospel and her testimony has brought many to the church.

The terrible disease of leprosy plagued Sunare Kumallo for many years. She came to the church in Hagereselam and received cleansing for her body and salvation for her soul, and faithfully serves God with overflowing joy since that day.

Defarsa Ruksso had suffered total blindness for twelve years when his family led him to the Teticha Apostolic church in 1977. His healing sparked the opening of three new churches, and he pastors one of them where miracles are the daily fare in every service.

Possessed by the devil, lame in both legs and dumb for a year, Lema Tonna became a prisoner in his own house. His family got fed up looking for cures and carried him to the Hagereselam Apostolic church for prayer. The devil had to go. Lema walked and could speak again and wholly followed the Lord. His healing caused the opening of a new church at Hitolle which now has over 140 members.

Poor insane Kebebush Bekele wandered up and down in Hagereselam sleeping wherever nightfall found her. Two of her relatives heard that many insane people had been healed at the Apostolic church; they brought her September 11, 1992 and she received instant healing and a restored mind through prayer. Today, she is normal and happy living a spiritual life.

Metto Fakie slept in the streets and wandered yelling through the villages and the bush during his twelve years of insanity. When he stabbed himself in the stomach with a sharp knife, his family took him to the hospital until the wound healed, and then brought him to Hagereselam where strong prayers restored his mind and saved his soul in 1990. This inspired the beginning of a new church at Awara Galade with no less than 130 saints.

Wollayta

The SIM started in Wollayta before the Italian invasion in 1926, and have a membership of approximately one million. Because they are more civilized and better educated than most of us, they have considerable power under the Derg Regime in the towns and peasant associations. The SIM priests, determined to keep the monopoly on religion, have bitterly opposed the churches established by our brothers. They bribed the Derg to close our churches and caused Dawit and others to go to jail. Brother Dawit seemed to spend most of his time getting arrested, thrown in jail, and being released.

They closed the church built by Brother Wendell in Gachano and confiscated the property of Brother Dibessa, took the church's roofing, and arrested him. They tried to send Hezkiel and other young men to the battlefield which could only be avoided by paying an escalating bribe starting at 100 Birr and finally went to 500 Birr. Those who could not pay stayed in prison. Some leaders taunted the young men with, "Why don't you pay with the American dollars they send you and get out of this place?"

A SIM member who got converted in the Apostolic church gave this testimony:

We set out to eliminate Brother Dawit. We had 738 churches with pastors, and we thought it would be easy to destroy Dawit and close the Soddo Apostolic church. But the stick we used against Dawit struck us. It happened like this: We had a course in 1983 called `Teaching of Divinity' which recommended a division between the state and the church. Several phrases denounced the leaders of the country, and one sentence read, `The church is ready to be slaughtered.' This course was duplicated and widely distributed in the whole province. When members of the Derg read this, in spite of our men with political power from local authorities to provincial offices, they struck immediately and closed all our churches. We ourselves destroyed our churches; it is the judgment of God who revealed our sins.

The Derg only closed the Apostolic churches; they totally destroyed the SIM church buildings and either used the roofing for political offices or divided them among the wrecking crews. It is a small thing that the SIM exposed our saints to prison and suffering--they counted it all joy. Besides, we baptized 120 of their preachers and all the members they pastored in the name of Jesus. Those who did not come to us have split into two or three divisions most of whom labor under various delusions.

In every case, those who oppose us have received Satan as an angel of light. One group taught they would never die; consequently, when the son of a member died, they buried him secretly in their house. The authorities heard about it, dug up the body, and buried it openly in the graveyard shaming their error.

A merchant listened to the evil one's voice who first told him, "Fast, until I tell you to stop;" and then later, "Don't eat any more food for it grows in the earth that is cursed." When the horrible stench impelled his neighbors to break down his door to investigate, they found his body disintegrating. He had used his money--about 15,000 bir as toilet paper.

If our lives are not based on truth and the Apostles's doctrine, we are in danger.

Every conference held in Wollayta has been opposed by the other churches which schedule meetings to keep people from coming to us. They never stop trying to hurt me. We booked the stadium for our December, 1992 conference. Some of them hurried to get it on our dates, but the administrator said, "You cannot have it, we have given it to the Apostolic church."

Upset and angry, they called for their prophets to prophesy against us. They proclaimed loudly, "I will disperse them with snow and thunder and will kill them."

When the day came, snow, thunder, and rain came but the wind blew it all away with no harm done. The people of the town said, "What a wonderful thing!" while the false prophets hung their heads in shame.

Satan attacked Mulu, a tenth grade student and member of the Full Gospel Church. She lay on her bed unable to speak in January 1986. Sister Aberash Godano heard of her plight and called us. When we prayed in the name of Jesus, He delivered her.

Sister Emote (my wife) and I became seriously ill with a disease that sometimes seemed like malaria, other times like typhoid or pneumonia. Everyone in the Sodo church prayed for us, but twice we had to rush Sister Emote to the hospital. Medications did not help. After battling for a month I decided we needed extra prayer; I called Sister Erkenesh and she promised to gather the saints to intercede for our healing. Both of us recovered completely the same night and could go on with our ministry.

Terefe Tesfaye suffered such an assault from the devil that he lost his mind and his family took him to an Orthodox Monastery for a month. When this failed to cure him, they looked for charity to take him to a place of holy water in Yirgalem. Someone witnessed to him, and he decided to come to us. It took him three hours to stagger one kilometer to the church. He trembled as he told us about his problems, but they ended a few minutes later when we rebuked the devil who came out of him screaming. With complete healing, he desired baptism and received the Holy Ghost and became a blessed brother in our church. His wife and children have wholly followed the Lord because of his transformation.

Forty-six year old Tseghe Tadesse became possessed by Satan in her childhood in Sellale province, Shoa Region, where she grew up. She suffered all those years and made life miserable for her husband, Gutta Garedew, a driver for Sodo City council. His unhappy home life made him eager to obey the good news of the gospel. Coming to be baptized, he brought his very sick wife for prayer. When we rebuked the devil, he answered boastfully about the way he had afflicted her; however, by the power in the name of Jesus he had to depart. Both of them received the power of God and today Sister Tseghe Tadesse is one of our faithful leaders in the Ladies Auxiliary.

Their son who had not been able to speak since his childhood received a mighty deliverance after his parents came to the truth and God also healed his lame hand.

Tirgo Wadillo suffered from demon possession for years. In 1987 her mother and sister brought her to church for prayer. Delivered and healed, she gladly serves the Lord today.

Fanaye Desta had a life of utmost misery under Satan's rule. He threw her down often and she wallowed and foamed at the mouth, sometimes appearing more dead than alive. Her mother frantically took her from magicians to holy water places to monasteries until in vain she spent all her money. She had started selling her gold jewelry to try more cures when her nephew Brother Lewetegn told her the good news about Jesus the Healer and Deliverer. They came to the church and found restoration for her daughter and full and free salvation for both of them. The Lord also provided a good job in a government organization to supply their needs.

Brother Simeom Menna, converted in 1986, served God with courage though his demon-possessed wife, Wubitu Haile, gave him much sorrow. She often fell to the floor in severe convulsions and could find no rest neither day nor night. She often ran away from home and refused to feed her first child, but her husband's strong faith in Jesus not only brought her complete healing but delivered their son Yohannes from the hand of Satan. Today they walk in truth and serve God joyfully together.

A serious disease in her right hand left Sister Zenasa Kabeto unable to use the hand. She had pain, but no feeling in her fingers. During a Ladies' Wednesday prayer service when we offered prayers for the sick, she received her healing and is now the secretary and treasurer of the Ladies

Auxiliary Division of Wollayta section.

On a Wednesday of fasting and prayer the Lord healed Aster Fiku from long-standing acute pain in her leg.

Brother Gezahegn Gedda, deacon and secretary of the Youth division, is an employee of the government. He took a seriously high fever, and Sister Emote and I went to his home and rebuked the disease in Jesus name. He received instant healing.

High fever laid low three times a High School teacher, Brother Amha Awoke, and the name of Jesus healed him each time. He is a deacon and faithful member of Sodo Apostolic church.

Barza Bassa's binding addiction to tobacco and strong drink bothered him; he made vows to many gods trying to get free, but nothing helped. One day he spent most of his wages, 90 Birr for alcohol and tej and came home with only 7 Birr. He awoke sober and disgusted the next morning and decided, "My case is hopeless," and took a rope to hang himself. Fortunately, his wife wakened in time to call the neighbors for help and saved him from suicide. When one of them witnessed to him, he came to the church, got rid of his addiction through prayer and received salvation that day.

When Samuel Garedew got baptized in the name of Jesus and received the Holy Ghost in 1986, the Lord healed him of severe migraine headaches. He is a driver and praises God for protecting him from threatening accidents that seemed impossible to avoid, yet he came out unscathed each time.

In 1987 Brother Gutta Garedew learned more of God's power in two accidents, one on the banks of Buge river, the other near Addilo river, both caused by the mistakes of careless drivers. Only the hand of God prevented him plunging over the cliffs to certain death in each instance. In a hotel where Brother Garedew stayed the next year, a man became sick and died. He commanded the soul to return to the man's body in Jesus name and the man got up well. Later the same year as he drove a large truck loaded with logs and ten men sitting on top of the logs, the chains broke and the logs fell off. The men landed in a ditch with the logs on top of them, but no one got hurt.

The baby's name Hayawner Zeleke means "You are alive." One day his parents rushed him to the Sodo hospital suffering from meningitis. Before long the doctors said, "Take the baby home to die; he cannot live." They went home sadly to wait for their little one's death. His father made arrangements for the mourners to wail his passing, but his mother who knew the Lord sent a message to the church. When prayer went to the throne, Jesus raised the child up. Soon they saw him walking everywhere, healthy and strong.

Hundreds of temporary churches going up

CHAPTER SIXTEEN

SODO

By Dawitt

Though the church began in Sodo town in 1970 through the witness of Samuel Jejerso and Bessa Wondebo, persecution wiped it out two years later. By 1973 only two or three saints remained. My employment took me there in 1974. I rented a house and ministered to a few townsfolk and some who came in from the countryside. In 1975 the church sent me back to pastor; the congregation had diminished from a hundred or so to five.

Ato Bebock Gejabbo opened his home for a place of worship until 1978 when the government granted us a compound. As we prepared to build, persecution escalated, and false reports by our enemies put four of the saints and me in jail for over a month. Freed, we built our house and held church there until the completion of the new church in 1980, made possible by a gift from Bobbye Wendell.

People envious of our new building and the conversion of many souls stirred up a new persecution and the government confiscated the new church a year later.

Applications to regain the church building failed, but the work grew rapidly in our living room.

Freedom to worship ended again temporarily as I went to jail for three months after the second Minister's conference held in our compound in 1983 ministered to by Brothers Ayele Lakew and Degu Kekedi.

Brother Tekle brought us big blessings with the Word in a general conference held in our compound. Two months later the police arrested Brother Mengistu Meskale and me for preaching the gospel; we spent over three months in jail. In spite of these hindrances, hungry souls obeyed the gospel.

The December 1986 General Conference enjoyed the anointed ministry of Brother Tekle and Sister Erkenesh. We had to build temporary shelters for our Christmas celebration since our house could no longer hold all who came.

For the early 1987 Conference we had to construct a shelter big enough to accommodate seven hundred people as brethren came from many places. Unlimited blessings enriched our fellowship, and echoes of Holy Ghost singing flowed through the whole town. By this time the local church had outgrown our house, so we continued meetings in the shelter. At the December Conference the same year, the shelter had to be enlarged by half.

Those who seized our church had educational seminars in it for just two months. It remained closed several years, used only for storage. Because they did not set a guard or watchman thieves broke one of the doors and many windows. Later thieves took the shutters and the stored goods disappeared. I went continuously to the regional office applying for the return of our church, but they paid no attention to my pleas. We appealed to heaven; for three years the elders of the church met together three days a week for intercessory prayer and God gave us a promise, "I will bring again the captivity of Jacob's tents."

On April 3, 1988 after the Sunday morning service, an urgent call for afternoon prayer brought half of the saints with their children back to pray. A sudden heavy rain accompanied by strong, cold wind struck us and with one consent we took our only alternative and rushed in the church hall. Never had the Spirit fallen on us as it fell for the next hour--resurrection day for Sodo Church!

From that day we have worshiped the Lord freely in our church and our numbers increased from day to day to the extent we had to hold services in shifts. The work that started in 1976 with five reached five hundred in 1987. Growth did not come easy. The Sodo Church went through water and fire, but we thank God who brought us through with victory.

I pastored this work for thirteen years. Let me share some of the miracles Jesus did.

Once in jail, a policeman named Wolday had a serious ear infection. He took me out of my cell and told me about his problem. I poured a few drops of water in his ear and prayed for him; Jesus healed him that night.

While Brother Mengistu and I shared a prison cell, the chief of the prisoners (also a prisoner) hated us and constantly abused us verbally. When he became deathly ill, we prayed for him and Jesus healed him. Another day, he wakened me at 2:00 A.M. and took me to a prisoner hovering at the point of death. I laid my hands on him and rebuked the disease in the name of Jesus and daylight found him well. A demon-possessed and very sick prisoner disturbed everyone screaming with nightmares until we cast the devil out of him and prayed till healing came.

A Orthodox church leader and retired judge rejected the gospel when he heard it and immediately demons attacked his daughter. He took her to the monastery where the monks and workers prayed for her twenty days with no results. He called us to his house and deliverance came that day when we called on the name of Jesus.

Sister Wudnesh Takesso's arms and legs first became extremely cold, then useless, but prayer in the name of Jesus fulled restored her in 1987.

A doctor's eleven year-old daughter, Fetlework Deboch, suffered debilitating bouts of high fever from the age of eight, though her father took her from doctor to doctor and hospital to hospital without finding a cure or a cause for her illness. Her mother secretly wrapped her in a blanket and carried her on her back to the church and one simple prayer made her completely well.

Brother Bezuayehu Wolde Micheal, a university student, came to Sodo during vacation to spend the night with a relative. During the night sword-sharp pains pierced the right side of his body from his chest to his loin. I answered their call the next morning. With anointing oil and prayer in the name of Jesus instant healing came.

CHAPTER SEVENTEEN

LIGHT IN THE EVENING TIME

Papa Toshe Bechu's Story

I grew up in a family where the power of sin reigned supreme. My father, brothers, and all my relatives operated as magicians, sorcerers, and diviners sacrificing to demons. I inherited this evil and received extensive training in it, knowing no alternatives.

I asked my father to give me a virgin piece of land so I could make my own sacrifices to Satan. What a cruel master he is! Satan rewarded my service to him with unlimited poverty, distress, suffering of spirit, soul and body.

From childhood a dreadful disease shackled me that grew progressively worse from day to day. My family got weary of caring for me and when their efforts at cures failed they almost abandoned me. I lost weight until I became skin and bones and could not even turn over in the bed. They fastened two ropes to the roof rafters to help me change my position in the bed.

In a period of slight improvement I married. In spite

of a generous inheritance, my poor wife did not realize the hard road that lay ahead of her. In nine years of suffering, I vainly spent my wealth for medication and any food or drink the magicians said would help. I lay on ashes and tried many absurd remedies hoping for relief, but found none.

We declined from abundance to total poverty. After we came to the place we had nothing left to buy food to put on our table I cried bitterly to the Lord, "Why do you not heal me? Oh, my Creator, either heal me of kill me."

On Thursday after that prayer, I had a vision: it seemed an angel took me to heaven. I heard God ask, *Have you brought the man who entreated me to either heal him or kill him?*

Yes, the angel answered.

Take him to the lesson room.

In that room a teacher held a large book open against his chest so I could see the writing. Though I am illiterate, and had never seen the alphabet before, when he fastened his eyes on me I could read the book and understand the words. When he turned his face away from me, the words disappeared and I couldn't remember what I read.

After I lay some time at his feet I rolled under a curtain in the judgement room where three angels sat to judge me. Laying before them I asked, "Please tell me what mistakes have caused my suffering for nine years. Let me hear and die, or, otherwise, pardon me and let me be healed."

The angels talked to each other and one said, *His iniquity is not so great he cannot be forgiven. Release him and let him go.*

Young man, one of them said, *do not sacrifice to devils, do not divine or be a wizard. Do not steal or give false witness or commit adultery. When called to witness boundaries, do not favor family or friend, show the boundaries in truth. Worship God only who is Jesus Christ. If you keep these commandments you will live to be an old man.* Over and over he repeated, *Worship only god who is Jesus Christ.* Then he said, *Go!*

"Which way must I go?" I asked and he showed me a winding road.

As I walked three demons met me and asked, "What lessons did they give you?"

I told them the commandments of God given to me. They tried to destroy the words, but I said, "I will not listen to you," and continued on my way home.

When I regained consciousness I found my wife and a neighbor lady had sat by my bed over half a day expecting my death at any minute. My wife asked, "Will you try to drink a little milk?"

"Yes," I answered, "and not only milk, bring me some food."

Then I saw the goat tied to a log near the head of my bed on the instruction of a wizard and said, "First you must release the goat, I will not eat until you take that goat out of here."

She cried, "You have lost your mind. I don't want you to die, and if I untie the goat you will because the medicine the wizard put on it will kill you."

I remained hungry. My brother came to see me Friday morning. I told him, "I am healed, but will you please take away this goat?"

Shocked by my request he refused and left. Too weak to get up and untie the goat, I feel like I am beaten by a big whip of hunger. I knew my strength would return if I could eat, but I refused to compromise with the wizard's goat.

My oldest sister came to see me on Saturday. Knowing her habitual kindness, I thought surely she will help me. but she answered, "Your father, brothers, and sisters have died; are you better than they? you will die anyway, but if you touch that goat you will die an evil death. why don't you just die peacefully?"

I understood everyone feared to help me, and I wept sorely thinking I will surely die. then I asked God to give me wisdom to release the goat and he did. I asked my wife to make me a bed on the floor near the goat and she did. With the aid of the rope I reached the log and called for God's help. I pulled it toward me with my hands and pushed it away with my feet; it broke in half and fell on me setting the goat free.

The people feared to let it go and tied it near my feet. I felt released and ate the food my wife brought me. Every day I grew stronger and fifteen days I attended the funeral of friend using only a staff to support me. With a nephew's help, I grew bold and slaughtered the fat goat.

Satan does not sleep. He is our worst enemy, and he cheated me out of the divine revelation of God's name. Since I could not remember His name, I called him "Kitos". For a year I told everyone about my God "Kitos" who healed me and told me to worship Him.

One day as I worked in my garden a friend came to see me and told me about the religion that healed his brother. He took me to that church and I found again the true name of my God, Jesus Christ. I heard the gospel preached and believed; immediately they baptized me in the titles, Father, Son and Holy Ghost. (This is one regret I have --none of us understood the oneness of God.) I became a leader in that church and taught all I knew, baptizing many people the same way for fifty-two years. But Jesus loves me and by His great mercy I have been baptized in the name of Jesus this year...I am eighty-eight years old.

For the earth shall be filled with the knowledge of the glory of the Lord, as the waters cover the sea (Habakkuk 2:14).

TESTIMONY OF JEGERIE JELAMO

I was born in Gacheno region, Wollayta Province. We lived in spiritual darkness, but as a lad tending my father's cattle in the wide fields, God put a desire in my heart to know Him. Every day as I herded the cows toward the grass, I looked right and left to be sure no one listened and prayed the same prayers over and over lifting my hands toward heaven;

My Creator please reveal yourself to me. If you reveal yourself to me, I will worship you alone.

Oh God, don't allow me to covet the wealth of others.

Please God, do not let me become jealous, lead me on the true path.

Who are you that created my hands with fingers and gave me strong legs and feet?

God, give me medicine for death because I want to live forever.

If you are the true God, please give me a wife who has no parents, because she might depend on her parents and quarrel with me.

I continued my prayers for some time. One day God revealed himself to me in a brilliant light. He came to me in dreams and visions, saying *I am Jesus*. I bowed with my forehead to the ground and prayed this prayer with my whole heart, *Send me Your Word and I will obey it.*

I began to preach while still young about the God who revealed Himself to me and many people believed. My parents died in my childhood and God gave me a wife who lost her parents at an early age. We have been married for fifty-two years and have never quarreled.

After my revelation came, I heard of people who preached Jesus. I went to them and worked with that denomination for forty-five years.. Because I did not understand the truth of one God, I baptized thousands of people in the name of the Father, Son, and Holy Ghost, the same way I had been baptized. Now God has swept all confusion from my mind and revealed the glorious truth to me. In my old age I have been baptized in the name of Jesus and filled with the Holy Ghost and joyfully minister His gospel even though I am eighty-six years old.

Tekle adds: Papa Jegerie, the descendant of Tona, King of Wollayta, is very influential and has witnessed to many of his peers, old men, who preached for fifty years and now follow the truth. He founded the SIM in his area and because he now walks in the Light, their leaders are disturbed as a house whose foundation is moved.

TESTIMONY OF PAPA GODEBO ADARE

God's Word tells of many who thought they knew God and zealously persecuted and killed the prophets sent by the Lord. Seldom does one so misguided come to the truth as the Apostle Paul did--struck down on the Damascus road. I am one of them who have obeyed truth, though I came the hard way.

I ministered in Waritta Locale, Wollayta section for the John the Baptist religion for fifty-two years. For the last five years, my son Hezkiel has witnessed to me continually, saying, "Please believe in the true God." Each time I answered, "Am I not believing in a God?"

He brought many evangelists with him to talk to me, but I hardened my heart. Often when they spoke to me strongly, I rejected their words and threatened, "I should take you to the police, but for God's sake, I will pardon you. Now, get out of my house."

One of my three hundred members lay dying and I went with others to pray for him. When I stood after my prayer, an unseen power jerked my Bible out of my hands upwards. I jumped up and grabbed it saying, "How dare you take the book from me, a servant of Jesus Christ?"

The force lifted me to the ceiling and threw me on the floor and it seemed my spirit dissolved within me. The villagers carried me home and the next day, thinking I am about to die, I made my last will and testament. While I am busy with this a voice spoke, *Why do you distribute your money? You will not die.* I turned to find the speaker and could see no one.

He spoke again, *Do not give your property to anyone, you will use it yourself. You will not die.* The voice sounded the same, but I could not see Him.

After that my son came again and said, "Dad, if you believe, you will be saved."

I replied angrily, "No, I do not believe. Do you mean that the one I believe in is not a God?" He tried for three days to convince me and went away defeated.

A week later, a divine voice gave me a decree in my sleep: *Pass quickly!* I could not understand, but when this continued for fifteen days I felt the Lord is telling me I must pass quickly to the Apostolic church. I called my son and he took me to a pastor who baptized me in the name of Jesus for the remission of my sins and by the wonderful mercy of the Lord, He filled me with the Holy Ghost. It came exactly as He poured it out on the Apostles in Acts, Chapter Two. What joy has filled my life! May His holy name be forever blessed.

Welcoming crowd at country church

CHAPTER EIGHTEEN

MORE MIRACLES

Another worker answers the call!

While I worked in Awassa town in the engineering department I went to a Wednesday all-night fellowship and heard Brother Tekle give a powerful message on stepping out in the ministry. Though I finally found what I searched for all my life, I did not consider going full-time in the ministry because of my spiritual background.

I started out as a teacher with the SIM which I left because I felt no satisfaction in my heart. I became a preacher in the Adventist church; that did not satisfy my inner longings, so I joined the Orthodox Church thinking I had found the old truth. From that confusion I went to the book of Acts salvation which brought me a new dimension of God and His Word.

For some time a voice kept repeating in my heart, *Forget everything else, preach the gospel. Go out and win souls.* This troubled me and I prayed all night after Tekle's sermon. As I continued in prayer, the Spirit moved through me mightily and I heard these words distinctly, *Go out in the ministry of the gospel.*"

I found it hard to believe and said, "If this is true, let it come through Brother Tekle or Sister Erkenesh."

When I went to the Friday night service Brother Tekle said, "Don't leave; Sister Erkenesh has a message for you." She confirmed what the Lord had told me. Even though my heart accepted it, I feared the people would not accept me. I wondered whether it would be best if I went to Sidamo where my past is not known?

I asked the Lord for a sign showing me where He wanted me to labor and He answered with a vision of the families who would be saved in Wollayta. Again, I prayed, *Please confirm this by my leaders.* The next day I went to pray in a cave in Mount Tabor and heard a loud voice say, *You will hear your answer from Brother Tekle.*

I hurried to the Wednesday evening service and Bro. Tekle said, "You must go to Wollayta to begin your ministry. Joy filled my heart. With all doubts banished, I knelt before Brother Tekle for prayer and when he prayed the Holy Ghost lit up my heart.

I resigned my job saying, "Jesus will be my salary." The next day I took my family to Wollayta and God opened a door for me. Revival has blessed our efforts and we have enlarged the church several times and opened twenty branch works from my congregation. We have established one hundred and twenty churches. Soon after my move to Wollayta Brother Tekle shared with me the grand spiritual truths of salvation and baptized me in the name of Jesus. I rejoice to be a servant of that One mighty God.

Her family brought Genie Gemagna to our church; she had crawled on her belly like a snake for four years. I told the family, "If you believe, she will be healed." I rebuked the disease and she immediately stood up. Her conversion brought many of the villagers to the church.

Zecharias Gagaba lost his mind and if his family did not keep him tied to a tree he would run away. One prayer in the name of Jesus restored him and they released him from the log.

Doctors at the hospital told the family of Germem Gantd to take him home since he could not live. By the time they brought him to me he had died and the body looked horrible. Even though they wanted to hurry on, we gave them some Bible teaching before we prayed for him without expecting an answer. But instantly his life returned and he sat up. His rising from the dead brought many souls to salvation.

Hunchback Alemu Assaro got sick unto death and his family brought him to me for prayer. As I called on the Lord, the demon in him screamed and made him wallow on the floor until it knocked him out. He appeared dead, then before our eyes he stood up with a straight back healed of his sickness. Even better than healing, he found the joys of salvation and became a dynamic soul-winner.

Ansom Amajo suffered a strange disorder; with her body bent double and her arms and legs intertwined, she looked pitiful. Along with her physical problems, her mind seemed confused. We went to her house to witness and learned that would-be healers had forbidden her to eat food or drink water for six months (she had not fully obeyed those weird instructions).

With our first prayer, her mind cleared and we talked to her about the Word of God. We said, "Call on the name of Jesus and He will heal you."

As she cried to Jesus repeatedly, He straightened her

body and healed her. She could wear clothes again and came to church the following sunday to be baptized in Jesus name. She received the Holy Ghost and is a faithful servant of the Lord.

The Work in Bale

By Pastor Lencha

One day in my garden I felt like praying, but my mouth closed tightly and I couldn't open it for half an hour. Finally, I prayed in my heart: *Oh, Jesus, show me Your way.*

Three days later my heart leaped within me as I read Acts 2:1-4; a loud voice in my ear said, *Didn't you ask me to show you my way?* I understood the God of heaven is leading me, though I did not know what to do. He sent sister Emote Wadisso to my house to open the Word to me; it agreed with the vision and I believed.

I knew I had to be baptized, but I delayed three months. Instructions came clearly in a night vision. *Is cold food good to eat? Arise and be baptized in my name!* I prayed four hours begging the Lord, *Please don't come before I can get baptized.* I walked eight hours to get to Dawit Toshe's house to be baptized and asked him to make it as quickly as possible. The sight of the river delighted me. I hurried into the water and put on Christ. It seemed like paradise to have my sins remitted in His name and I rejoiced with all my might.

The church gave me the responsibility of taking this God-revealed gospel to my district. In 1979 my family and I prayed and witnessed alone. Other denominations rejected us from all social activities and persecuted us. Even my mother refused to accept my witness.

On my return from a three day journey I saw a large crowd mourning at my house and heard the sad news, "Your mother is dead." I entered the house weeping and fell on my knees, "Oh Lord, you know we have no place to bury our dead. How can I carry this heavy load? What can I do? What is your plan for us today?"

The Holy Ghost touched me and I called the mourners together and told them, "Stand up and pray." The willing ones stood with me while I interceded for an hour. Then my mother spoke and after a few minutes sat up.

I said, "See how God works!" and began to walk up and down and preached to the mourners in the house and in the yard. This miracle opened many doors.

On my way to another town, I heard a voice say, *Go to Kindo Angalla.* I looked right and left and saw no one, but the voice came again, *Go to Kindo Angalla.* Even though night approached, the moon shone brightly and I walked the nine hour journey easily. On my arrival I found ten brethren and we began to sing, "Go Fish for Men" on the street. The villagers came to hear the gospel and thirty-five of them got baptized in Jesus name and received the Holy Ghost.

Four men carried a lame man on a stretcher, asking prayer. When we prayed, he jumped off the stretcher and began leaping and praising God. He walked to his home that night.

Today, Kindo Angalla has six churches with their own pastors and the people's ears are open to the gospel.

As one of our saints travelled to Keffa he saw a man in a village hemorrhaging violently. He called for oil, anointed him and prayed. The blood stopped immediately. He witnessed to the amazed people and found them hungry for God. We have now built three churches in that area from the fruit of that witness.

Brother Tekle wrote a tract titled, *Do You Want to Be Saved?* I gave a copy to a communist teacher; it made him so angry he threw it away and lent his Bible to some one to get it out of his house. He then displayed bulletins and books of the revolution prominently in attractive folders. That night as he slept an angel beat him with a big whip, saying, *You put the word of men in a nice flolder; what did you do with the Word of God?*

Early the next morning he sent a message to one of the saints, "Because I threw away the tract, an angel beat me all night. I want Lencha; where is he?"

Since other commitments detained me, I couldn't go but I sent a message, "If it is the Lord, you will be beaten again tonight; if it is Satan, he will not return."

With a troubled heart, he asked his wife to help him and they searched in vain the whole night for the tract. The next morning he said, "I may die today, swallowed by fear if I don't do something. I've got to see Lencha."

We got together that day and when I explained the gospel he gladly obeyed and today, no longer a communist, he lives as a friend of God.

Wheelage

Gifted to witness, Sister Maria won her sister and her mother, Tijube. Because of her, several full Gospel preachers gathered at Tijube's house for a meeting with Brother Ejigu in Hawa Gallen, Kelem District. The police interrupted the service and took all of them to jail. Brother Ejigu rejoiced over ample time to teach the doctrine of Jesus in its glorious fullness. Soon, the preachers became eager for baptism in the name of Jesus and asked, "What can we do?"

Wisdom instructed Brother Ejigu, "We will ask permission for an escort to take us to the river because we want to bathe and wash our clothes, and I can baptize you then."

God gave them favor and a small gift of money took away their escort's desire to hurry and the preachers felt grateful for freedom to obey the Lord. Back in the prison things got worse. The police did not allow the prisoners to eat and tortured their feet with rods.

The next day they forced them to walk on those bruised feet and work on road construction. Returning from work, the guards made them slide on their stomachs like a snake.

Maria's husband, Ato Abdissa, a highly respected man, felt grieved over the inhuman treatment of the preachers and applied to the authorities to settle the case. The court's verdict; ninety Birr each or three months in jail, but the church paid the fines and the men had liberty to launch revival in that area. One of the men, Solomon Terfa is a leader and has founded many churches.

Erkenesh with Zebiba directed by an angel walked 120 K to the church. Now saved and a soul winner.

Crippled boy healed

Joyous welcome

CHAPTER NINETEEN

A REPORT TO TEKLEMARIAM

We bring to your attention the wonders and miracles done in the name of Jesus Christ that contributed to the growth of the church in Denbidolo sub-section.

Realizing the seriousness of her condition the saints and neighbors felt troubled, wondering how and where Sister Workinesh Danssi could be buried if she did not live. When she died July 28, 1990, Brother Solomon and a committee went to the Provincial office to apply for a burial place. They received the curt reply, "We have no place for you to bury your dead."

Twenty-four hours had passed by the time they returned and fell on their faces seeking an answer from Jesus. While they prayed, life returned to the cold body and Sister Workinesh stood up alive and well. This astonishing miracle moved the hearts of many heathen to obey the gospel. The lady is an ardent worker in the church today.

The daughter of Gobena Geleta served God faithfully and sang in the local Apostolic church choir. When she came home from choir practice one day, her father beat her so severely she ran to the church for protection. He followed her with a spear determined to kill her. The pastor jumped between the girl and her father; he then lifted his spear to kill the pastor, but soldiers came just in time to save his life.

Frustrated Gobena went home and suddenly became desperately sick. His heathen neighbors tried to treat him with various remedies; when nothing helped they decided to take him to the hospital on a horse, but the horse refused to move. They carried him back in his house and he grew steadily worse. Finally in desperation he requested the brethren from the Apostolic church to come pray for him. One prayer brought him healing and a change of heart. When he came to church with a spear and a stone tied at his waist that he planned to throw, he said, "I have fought the Christians with these tools. Now I ask the leaders to loose me from them so I can follow Jesus." After his baptism in water and in the Spirit he has served the Lord faithfully doing whatever needs doing in the church.

From Wollayta, Brother Hezkiel felt led to go to Arba Minch and open a pharmacy-clinic. He found it a profitable place to witness. He took patients willing to listen to the Word to a private room where he taught them and prayed with them until they received the Holy Ghost and healing. Local church leaders hearing of this reported it to the communists and the trouble began. They arrested and released him many times, trying to force him to witness only .when off-duty.

During those persecutions, the people dared not respond to a greeting with *Praise the Lord, we are fine*, for they would be arrested. When anyone said *Good morning,* one must answer *Forward with our bitter struggle!* The saints went quietly at night, two by two to secret meetings careful not to sing loudly or draw attention with their worship.

In the beginning of the work, not being a qualified preacher, Hezkiel either took his converts to Wollayta for baptism or asked a preacher to come and baptize them. Not many of them desired even a brief visit in this dangerous area. Brother Tekle wisely decided the long-suffering Hezkiel qualified and the leaders of the church ordained him on July 4, 1982.

By this time his congregation numbered thirty- seven. A week after his ordination, as Hezkiel journeyed on a bus to mourn his uncle's death, God warned him with the memory of another minister's witness that Satan had attacked his saints with the same spirit of delusion Brother Samuel Jejersso had experienced. The words came: *Let the dead bury the dead. Instead of going to mourn for your uncle, return and save your church* .

Returning, he found a woman had given a prophecy by Satan saying, "I am Jesus, your God, and I will fill all of you with my Spirit by Sunday." When he walked into the church God gave him 2 Corinthians 11:14: *...for Satan himself is transformed into an angel of light.* He told the people, "Even though he called himself Jesus, Satan spoke to you to bring confusion."

When he rebuked the devil in that sister, she said, "We are legion, We became annoyed with this true gospel beginning so powerfully in this region so we came to deceive the people and destroy the work." They cast the devil out in the name of Jesus, and the believers agreed God gave them knowledge to understand Satan's work. The church is strengthened in the Spirit.

The church had purchased a hut at Limat Sefer for a place of worship, and planned for another fellowship a few weeks later. Hezkiel did not know his enemies learned the date and planned to raid the place, take all the believers to prison, and kill him; but he heard the voice of the Lord say, "Go to Addis." On the way he heard that his sister was critically ill, so he decided to return. As he sat in the bus he felt the Lord take him by the hand and say, "If I have told you to go, why will you return?" He quickly got off that bus and went to Addis to say goodby to Reverend Harris, missionary to Kenya who had served as Ethiopia's Superintendent for a time.

Many soldiers and revolutionary guards surrounded the hut to arrest the believers and kill Hezkiel--action planned against the supposed anti-revolutionaries. They stormed in shouting, "Where is that anti-revolutionary Pente leader?" After finding only twenty-seven students and day-laborers, they waited from 8:00 A.M. until 10:00 P.M. thinking Hezkiel would eventually come. When he didn't, they took everyone to jail. they despised their "catch" saying, "these are nothing." They went to the pharmacy and arrested the two people who managed it, then arrested his sister who Hezkiel left in charge of his house. With all the excitement, her illness disappeared and she phoned him the next day that COPWE, a political workers organization, had distributed "wanted" posters with his picture on it to all police checkpoints saying, "Arrest this man."

His sister suggested he stay away until God showed him His will. In two weeks they released the prisoners, confiscated the hut, and with intensified persecution forced the fellowship to meet secretly at different homes in small groups at night. Brother Hezkiel came to Wollayta to wait for God's will, and could only communicate with his saints by letters. Persecution followed him to Wollayta with a rumor, "This is the man who distributed the American dollars sent to the Pentes by the CIA for insurrection; he must be arrested before he corrupts the young people's minds."

For ten months Hezkiel hid here and there from his accusers. He spent fifteen days in Brother Mulat's kitchen, where they sneaked in a little food to keep him alive. With his enemies hot on his trail he went to Areka and stayed with Brother Gentu Gelesew. The Administrator found him there and arrested his host for a day saying, "Why do you shelter this Pente leader who has turned Arba Minch up-side-down?" Hezkiel slipped away to Brother Ashe's place in Hanchuch.

Since the government confiscated his pharmacy, Hezkiel had no income, but he testified that all during this troublesome time, God miraculously provided for him and his family. Finally with the call renewed by Jesus saying, *I am still in control, go to Arba Minch*, he returned and encouraged the saints with his account of ten months of miracles and wonders.

Those imprisoned in Hezkiel's absence remained faithful and God increased the number of believers to fifty-five. A typist for the COPWE repented and wanted to be baptized. Hezkiel took her and six others who wanted to follow the Lord through the water to the river at ten o'clock at night. When soldiers who followed them secretly appeared with flashlights, Hezkiel encouraged his fearful flock with the story of soldiers who came to take Elisha as told in 2 Kings 6:15-19 and God struck them blind. "We have no alternative but to ask the Lord to close their eyes," Hezkiel said and led his little flock in prayer. The soldiers came near, shone their lights full on the pastor and his group standing in the water, and passed by without a word.

A short time later two women wanted baptism. They followed the river to its source hoping to avoid interference. With mission accomplished, sundown overtook them on the way home, and two girls joined them who had been hunting firewood. Unknowingly they took a short cut across the prison farm, and the guards raised their guns to kill these unknown intruders.(They had killed two thieves the day before on these grounds.) With uplifted gun, the guard yelled, "Halt! Who are you?" and the frightened girls wanted to run away.

Raising his hands toward heaven, Brother Hezkiel answered, "In Jesus name, we are men of God."

"What are you doing here this time of night?" one guard asked.

Before he could answer, another guard who knew Hezkiel answered for him, "They have come to hunt these girls who went to the forest to collect firewood and foolishly stayed too long."

He turned and rebuked the girls, "Why didn't you return in daylight hours? Why have you made a problem for this man by staying so late in the forest?"

The guards courteously escorted them to town.

The wife of a denominational minister became demon possessed at Woze Shara, a near-by rural area. Her husband brought her to Arba Munich seeking help and took her to a wizard. The wizard beat her with a whip trying to cure her, but it didn't help. One of the church sisters witnessed to her husband saying, "If you will believe Jesus and come to Him, He will heal you and your wife." She brought the man to Hezkiel who taught him the Word, and he received it with joy, requesting baptism immediately.

Afterward, Hezkiel took several believers with them

to go pray for the preacher's wife. When they bound the demon in the woman, other demons outside tried to help them by agitating unbelievers who ran to the police and reported, "Come quickly, the Pentes are praying at this house."

Brother Hezkiel told the man, "We will return later and finish this work; the Lord has warned me another problem is on the way."

As soon as they left, soldiers arrived and took control of the house and the surroundings. When they could find no Pentes, they took the wizard to jail, giving the believers and Brother Hezkiel a peaceful time to return and cast the devil out. Brother Daniel and his wife returned home rejoicing.

Hezkiel wanted to visit Daniel at Woze Shara. Since radical young revolutionaries patrolled the roads all day to prevent people going from one place to another they decided to go at night. His guide who had only been on the road once brought a big three-battery flashlight to help them find the way. When they left the town behind on their two-hour walk and entered the jungle, darkness seized them. They turned on the flashlight and its bulb burned out. In complete darkness they fumbled their way in a place of many cliffs, and followed a gorge thinking they had found the road. They slid helplessly in the sand until they fell at the foot of a cliff more than thirty feet high.

Brother Hezkiel lifted his voice to Jesus, "Oh Lord, in the daytime we trust the sun, but the sun has gone down leaving us alone in the darkness. We thought the three-battery flashlight could help us, but the bulb burned out. Since You are the light of the world and You never change, You are our only hope. By your miraculous power lead us to

Brother Daniel's house in Woze Shara." His fellow-travelers shared the fervent "Amen!"

They opened their eyes to see a white line easily visible on the ground. With gratitude Hezkiel said, "Walk on this line; it is the road to Brother Daniel's house." The line ended at his front door.

God gave them fruit for their labor; three people obeyed the gospel and so began the church at Woze Shara.

As Hezkiel walked down the road one night with his son Ayele and another brother on their way to a meeting on the farm, members of COPWE roughly grabbed them. They yelled to the workers, "Come help us; the Pentes will spoil our youth." The brother and his son slipped away from the mob, but they beat Hezkiel unmercifully. When they wanted to castrate him like an ox, recalling the scripture 2 Peter 2:19-23, he did not resist. God spared his life by one of the revolutionary leaders saying, "Wait. We must not kill him ourselves; we should hand him over to the law. We will detain him in our prison."

Some whispered among themselves, "We will return and finish this work later."

Ayele ran home and cried, "The COPWE are killing my father!" His oldest brother ALemayehu, a soldier on leave from the battle front, and some of the brothers hurried to report the attack to the police who sent an armed escort with them. When the police got there, they found the men outside boasting what they had done.

The police asked, "Where is Hezkiel who has been reported dead?"

The leader replied, "We haven't taken action against him, yet."

"This is illegal," said the police. "We stand against

injustice. Hand the man over to us peaceably, or we will take him by force."

When the men acquiesced they found Hezkiel nearer dead than alive and took him first to the police station for a statement, then to the hospital. After his recovery and much discussion back and forth between the police and the COPWE, the latter called him to their office to answer twelve questions. They gave him five days to go to Addis and get an answer from the headquarters church for their main question: Does the Apostolic church have a license to preach in this country?

Fortunately, Brother Tekle could give him a copy of the letter from the Security Office giving the Apostolic Church freedom of worship and granting them graveyards.

After Hezkiel's recovery his opponents backed away from open harassment, but they stirred up the Orthodox priests and local authorities against him. They started stoning his house day and night. His family could hardly sleep at night. Some of the rocks pierced the roof, but the police refused to respond to their calls for help. In spite of these things, a continual flow of hungry hearts came seeking God and his house could no longer hold them.

To avoid danger at the river, Hezkiel brought a man from another town to secretly build a baptismal tank in his house, but over-crowding became intolerable. After ten people sat on a table and broke it, they built a platform under the eucalyptus trees in Hezkiel's compound. Services continued outside when the weather permitted. A little later they built a bamboo shed which allowed the rain to fall through and make the ground muddy. Outsiders mocked the church under a tree.

After a heavy rain as the saints struggled in thick

mud, Hezkiel told them, "Jesus reasoned with me, `How can I fellowship with you in all this mud?'"

Some of the brothers thought they should roof the church with iron sheets, but as Hezkiel prayed for the church, the Lord reminded him of the hundred and twenty iron sheets forming the fence around the compound, "Your compound is well fenced with iron sheets, but my house is bamboo." Weeping, the pastor instructed his men to take the iron sheets for the hall and replace the fence with bamboo.

They needed wood for rafters which could not be bought without showing a plan which they did not have, but the Lord helped them bring a tall tree from the country side that served the purpose. Outsiders called it Hezkiel's service building.

Though Hezkiel had permission from the authorities to build the hall in his compound, the intimidators tried to destroy it. They brought a load of stones and threw them on the roof until they reached the point of exhaustion, while inside the people sang and received the Holy Ghost.

One day the Lord spoke through Hezkiel, *Since My name is rejected, I want you to build a beautiful building for the glory of My name.*

The men of the church planned a larger and more beautiful building in Hezkiel's compound and faced the same problem getting the needed wood. The Lord reassured them, *Even though you do not have a blue print, the heaven and the earth is mine. Be still and load the wood; I will take care of the checkpoints.*

Sure enough, at every checkpoint they simply said, *for the church* and the police removed the barriers and let them through.

They had not completely finished the church before

their opponents got permission to destroy the building. The church appealed and God used the Administrator who summed up the situation, "This is simply religious competition and no one is to tear down the church."

Since they have outgrown the hall anyway Hezkiel reminded the authorities of the letter from the Security Office and boldly asked for a place to build a church and a graveyard. He received both and enjoyed a short time of relative peace.

Getting ready to build, he bought stone to begin his church. The priests falsely accused him of stealing the stone from their churches and had him arrested. The court released him on surety, and the case drug on for four years.

During this time the Derg fell and EPRDF took over the country. Hezkiel had a relative high in politics who fell in disfavor. Hezkiel's enemies built fantasy on that fact and reported, "Hezkiel is an anti-revolutionary who is training young men to overthrow the government. He should be arrested and killed. These efforts failed because the EPRDF checked his records and found him blameless.

Then the Priests arranged a demonstration with the villagers who marched through town screaming as they denounced Hezkiel with slogan placards advising EPRDF to remove him.

God dispersed the parade with all their yelling like the wind, but in January 1989, enemies of the true gospel made another plan to eliminate Brother Hezkiel. Fearing to be accused of a crime if an individual killed him, they planned the dark deed for a holiday so the people could be the their scape goat. Epiphany is a widely celebrated holiday and they thought to dash in the church, disturb the program, kill Hezkiel, and escape in the confusion. They reckoned the church would scatter without their leader.

The devil told Hezkiel, "You will die; you shall surely die." He quoted Psalms 118:16-18 in reply, but as the opposing spirit increased, he began to think, "Maybe it is God's will for me to die in this place."

As he considered this, he decided he should let Brother Tekle know about this possibility. When he called and got no answer, he put Abraham Bore, pastor of Mesketo, in charge of the services and went to get a bus to Addis. Carrying a bag of clothes and a bag of money to turn in to headquarters, he missed both buses of the Addis schedules. He then took one to another town. Down the road the bus had a minor accident. Fearing a delay he changed to another bus in a hurry, but he forgot his money bag. This bus moved quickly and he rejoiced in the Lord for helping him get the faster one. Satan slyly said, "Why do you thank God? You left your money on the other bus."

Before he got alarmed, the Lord assured him, *Fear not, it will not be lost.*

Arriving at the next town, he got off the bus and saw the other one coming. He got on when it stopped and told the conductor about the lost bag.

"Is it red?" he asked.

"Yes." Hezkiel answered, and the man handed him his bag intact.

Service in Addis headquarters church blessed him. The speaker talked about baptism in water, but explained, "Water is not the only baptism. Sometimes we must go through a baptism of stones thrown at us, a baptism of abuse, a baptism of false accusations, a baptism of being despised, a baptism of pain, a baptism of crucifixion, a baptism of prison, and even a baptism of death.

"As water baptism will not be changed though the water is cold, these other baptisms will not be changed for our benefit. All of them come in the will of Jesus and we must prepare ourselves for He has promised to be with us all the way."

Hezkiel repented and caught the bus back to Arba Minch. Epiphany had passed but, on his return he learned the happenings of that night. Over two hundred believers gathered in the church; suddenly four hundred fifty men gathered outside the back of the church while the people worshiped God inside. Then half of the intruders stormed in searching for Hezkiel; when they couldn't find him, one of them shot Brother Abraham Bore three times in the chest, but the bullets wouldn't fire. He shot in the air and the gun worked fine.

The mob outside had begun to stone the door and break the windows, yelling, "Down with the Pentes!" When they heard the gun fire, they thought someone had come to help their victims and fled. At the same time the believers ran away in the darkness, though a few hid in Hezkiel's house next door.

Brother Hezkiel gathered his congregation and preached the sermon of many baptisms to them and they all repented for running away in the crisis. Soon with the expert aid of two brothers from Brother Dawit's church, Hezkiel built a splendid church on the hill the government gave him. The church can be seen from every direction and is a testimony to the power of Jesus. Included with the church is a guest room, service building, and offices. They received much prayer and material assistance from the mother church. A tremendous conference in 1992 brought out most of the town to hear the gospel and, among many others, university professors found salvation.

The Apostolic church of Ethiopia produced a fine young man named Degu Kebede, staunch in faith and doctrine. Honed by his graduation from the Life Tabernacle Bible College in Nairobi, Kenya, he serves as presbyter of Shoa Section. Degu is an excellent interpreter and has inspired the young people's division to raise money for the construction of churches in areas where money is scarce. Since the organization of the Youth Division in 1987, they have given $196,942.19 which represents considerable sacrifice. They have built twenty-two churches and helped with many needs.

Several people got baptized in Mirab Abaya. As members of the Productive Farming group lost interest and fell away, Brother Deku Debuld, through many trials and much opposition, stayed true and served the Lord with all his heart. God sent an evangelist, Brother Berhanu, from Arba Minch to sow the good seed of the gospel in Mirab Abaya, supported diligently by faithful Deku. Brother Berhanu has faced many hardships and severe trials in that new work in the wilderness; however, it is growing. Such evangelists are supported with food and transport from a five cent offering every Sunday from each member of the Apostolic church.

Brother Hezkiel baptized and taught Brother Abera, and in God's will he returned to his family's village with the gospel. Though he began with only five members, the SIM with their twelve thousand members called a conference and denounced him as a beast. Since the leaders of the SIM domineered both the political and religious offices the growth of the new church worried them enough, they forcibly drafted Abera in the militia hoping he would die on the battle field.

Impressed with his ability, his instructors sent Abera back to his own village to train draftees. He had no young men in the required age group in his church; his trainees came from the SIM families! Amazed at God's goodness, he did the required work and continued preaching and his church grew.

One day a young man, full of anger over Abera's preaching, came close to him and fired three bullets point-blank in his chest while Abera stood with up-lifted arms praising and worshiping the Lord. The young man turned and ran as though someone chased him to the police station and fell before an officer trembling as he blubbered, "I have killed Abera, the Pente!"

The police detained him while they investigated. The men who came found Abera cheerful and unhurt without a smell of gunfire about him. Witnesses said, "We saw the bullet explode on your chest! How could you escape unhurt?"

Abera answered, *The angel of the Lord encampeth round about them that fear him, and delivereth them* (Psalms 34:7). *The name of the Lord is a strong tower: the righteous run into it and are safe* (Proverbs 18;10). God sent his angels to catch the bullets!"

The Lord led Hezkiel to visit Gebrehiwot Bune who lived near the development farm. Gebrehiwot accepted the Word of God joyfully, but his blind wife refused asking, "What is wrong with our first faith?"

Undismayed, Gebrehiwot went to the river to be baptized in the name of Jesus for the remission of his sins. As the believers prayed for him to receive the Holy Ghost, they also prayed for his wife's blind eyes and suddenly she shouted, "I can see! I can see!" She rejoiced all the way to the river to be baptized.

When Gebrehiwot got the Holy Ghost the devil burned his three houses that contained all his property. Brothers from the church helped him build a new house with iron sheets. When his wife got the Holy Ghost, The Peasant Association decided to kill him and took him from his home to their office. In the meantime a misunderstanding flared between the farm workers and the officials. Gebrehiwot stood in the middle of the confusion and whispered, "In Jesus name". Officials started shooting at the workers; one died. They shot back and wounded two officials who died after being taken to the hospital. The name of Jesus protected the new convert and his family and he received a call to work for the Lord in Shella Mella.

Hezkiel had baptized four people in Shella Mella when he taught at Brother Paulos Tona's house earlier. He took Gebrehiwot and a couple of brethren with him to teach again, and six people believed and asked for baptism. But the leader of the local revolutionary guard stood and said, "I will not accept this because I believe God is Trinity."

Hezkiel answered gently, "Anyone to whom truth is revealed can be baptized in the name of Jesus Christ for the remission of his sin. If you do not understand this, feel free to go.

"I do not understand," the man replied angrily, "and I will go."

"Since the river is far and it is near 6:00 P.M. some of you should go take care of your cattle; when you return, we will all walk to the river together."

As soon as the people left. Brother Hezkiel said, "I feel an opposing spirit. Let us pray." Together they rebuked the opposing spirit. They waited long but the men who left did not return.

Paulos said, "Let me go and see what hinders the new believers."

The preacher and his helpers felt disturbed and even dizzy. He said, "Let's get out of this house." The African moon shone resplendently, but they saw a large Acacia tree near and went to stand in its shade.

They had barely found that cover, when they saw the angry guard return who had left in the heat of opposition. It seemed as if he had blown a trumpet and called the whole association saying, "We need to take these men into custody. They have brought Pente doctrines to disturb our society."

A large crowd of men, women, and soldiers carrying rods, swords, and rifles filled the house the group had vacated and many stood at the door unable to get in. The group saw plainly and heard all they said, "Where is that rebel? We will teach him a thing or two."

The listeners thanked God for rescuing them from this mess.

When the would-be attackers could find no rebels they got angry with the man who called them for nothing. After fifteen minutes he yelled, "Here are the men!" The people stormed together snarling, "We've got them now!" And when they saw no one they turned on the guard with insults and yells of "Liar! Liar!"

Hezkiel and his saints stood still, no one saw them, Paulos and the six new believers did not return. Silence reigned. One of the believers suggested, "Why don't we go back in the house?"

"Why should we go in when God said get out?" Hezkiel answered, "One of the brothers I baptized last year lives about an hour from here. We will trust Jesus to lead us to his house."

They found the brother's home without difficulty and a few minutes later, Brother Paulos and four of the baptismal candidates came. Brother Hezkiel baptized them that night. The next day they returned to Paulos's house for another service and baptized the other two, later returning to Arba Minch in peace.

Today, Brother Gebrehiwot leads a victorious church in Shella Mella where idolatry once prevailed.

Men with a burden for souls reached out to every area. The witness of Aselle Abate resulted in three churches in the Konso section and God raised up pastors to shepherd the flocks. Pastor Dasmawi Kusiya, conscripted to the battle field, finally returned safely after six years.

The Dita Zara church began by Sister Almaz Dida witnessing to her brother Abraham Dida when she came to visit him from Addis. Abraham went to Arba Minch to learn more; when he wanted to obey the Word, Brother Hezkiel baptized him in Jesus name. Five months later, Brother Hezkiel came to visit Abraham and baptized sixteen souls, ten of whom received the Holy Ghost. Today the church grows under the leadership of Abraham Dida.

Hezkiel and Berhanu Wachmo traveled 235 kilometers to Gofa and found Abera Zuma, who had separated himself from all churches, seeking the truth. He found it in the messages preached by the two brothers and obeyed the gospel along with six other men.

On their second journey, a denominational leader interrupted the service bringing in four strong men with rods in their hands. He said sternly, "Stop preaching this new religion here. We believe in Jesus and we don't need you or your gospel. Leave this place at once if you value your lives for many of our young people have sworn to beat you. Our elders have gone to report you to the local Administration and Revolutionary guards. If you refuse to leave, we do not care what happens to you."

With great boldness, Hezkiel read to them Acts 5:27-33 and 39-42 and declared, "Jesus Christ is the only God and Savior and we are witnesses for Him. We not only believe in Him, we have been baptized in His name for the remission of our sins according to Acts 2:38. The gospel the Apostles preached has been revealed to us and we will baptize everyone who repents in the name of Jesus Christ. We cast out devils, cleanse the lepers, heal the sick, and raise the dead in His name as He taught. We believe and witness before you the true gospel; we understand we should obey God rather than man. Be careful that you do not quarrel with the creator of heaven and earth.

"We are not afraid of your torture; we are ready to die for the name of Jesus and your persecution is a sign to us of our salvation. Our persecutors oppose the true teaching of Jesus and they will perish. We fear nothing, for Jesus is with us. Nothing you can do will shock us or stop us from preaching the true gospel. We will never retreat. We will continue to proclaim Jesus Christ is Lord and gives everyone full and free salvation who will accept it."

The intruders backed away from the preacher's fervor and left saying, "We will return." The conference continued two more days; no one came to hinder and the church in Gofa Sawla became firmly established. The fire of Apostolic faith now leaps from Province to district to every locality with power.

Preachers trained and commissioned

Another new church

CHAPTER TWENTY

WITNESSES WITH POWER

By an Eyewitness

People from many different areas are brought by God to Addis Ababa to find true salvation. They are strictly taught their responsibility to witness to their families and friends when they go to visit their home village or town. The headquarters church plays a large role in spreading the gospel all over the country.

The gospel is the powerful light of God and is spreading fast in Chelia Province. Those who have accepted the faith witness fervently to each other, and those who reject the truth fight the church with diligence. They have passed the stage of *don't greet them* and *don't go near them* to the stage of *beat them, arrest them, stop them at any cost.*

At a conference in Des Babis the nominal preachers met to insult us and curse us. When we heard about it we fell on our faces and prayed, "Lord, save these people from their wicked ways. Send a sign to show them they are wrong." As we prayed on a sunny day, lightening struck their conference and killed four of them. They had prayed for judgement to strike us, but it came to them instead.

In another place a group met to conspire against us and lightening struck the house and burned it, though none of the people suffered harm. Fair thinking folks began to say, "If thunder and lightening strikes the places where the people denounce the Apostolic Church, then the God of the Apostolics must be the real God."

Brother Mulugeta testified when they called another conference to protect their people from the Apostolics, the local authorities came armed with machine guns and bombs and surrounded them saying, "The followers of the Apostolic faith do not get drunk, but you are drunkards. The Apostolics do not steal, but you are thieves." After insulting and degrading them, they broke up the conference and said, "No one is allowed to preach here but the Apostolic Church."

A woman in that area possessed of unclean spirits had lived in sorcery for thirty-five years. She tried hospitals and holy waters often to find relief but only grew worse and lost all hope for recovery. The brothers went to her house to witness, but Satan spoke through her with threats, "You better watch out. I am a god and I will hurt you."

The believers continued praying and laid hands on her in Jesus name and the devil came out with a scream of anguish. She happily followed the Lord in baptism in water and received the Holy Spirit. Today she rejoices continually, "Praise God, I have been delivered from living death."

With the Derg's overthrow and its militia dispersed, desperate men sold their arms for food putting guns and bombs in the hands of the irresponsible. Some of them who before threw stones now threw bombs in our midst as we prayed. In God's marvelous goodness none of those bombs exploded to harm us.

The church at Tokilega had many enemies, but none so determined as Ato Chelkeba Feyssa. He attempted to throw a bomb in the middle of a prayer meeting, but it clung to his fingers and refused to be thrown though he tried repeatedly. He discarded the bomb and heaved a large stone at us that landed in the middle of the room without touching anyone. Thankful for miraculous protection, the saints laid their hands on the stone and prayed for the man who threw it. "Oh Lord, may the hands that threw this stone be lifted up to praise You. We long to see it. Amen."

Chelkeba's hands began swelling causing him much distress. After several days of agony he came to apologize to us and reconcile with the God of the Apostolics. He knelt on the floor at our feet, asked forgiveness with tears, and we joined with him to entreat Jesus for mercy. His hard heart changed. We baptized him in Jesus name and the God whose mercy is beyond understanding filled him with the Holy Spirit.

Accepting the call to Mecha Dendi, Brother Berhanu began witnessing fervently and the Lord accepted his ministry and granted revival in the town and the country side.

With the Derg overthrow by EPRDF, came a change of government policy; each tribe would govern themselves. Longstanding hatred and prejudice between tribes had often flared into petty conflict in this area. The Amhara oppressed the Oromo for years causing them to hate their religion, the Orthodox church. Now organized, the Oromo wanted to drive the Amharas out of their region. They burned Orthodox churches and slaughtered people in a rampage. Only the government's mediation prevented wholesale civil war and gave the Apostolic church a wide open door with the true gospel, in spite of fragile peace.

Considering the Oromo tribe heathen and idolaters, the arrogant Amhara used proverbs like *The sins of the Oromos cannot be cleansed with cold water, or even with hot water.* The churches among the Oromo produced no priests or spiritual leaders, so the arrival of an Oromo who is also a Reverend expounding the Word of God in the Oromo language brought consternation.

The older religions immediately mobilized to fight Brother Berhanu. An Orthodox priest incited the people with violent words, "Stand for your religion to the shedding of blood."

This incited his fanatical members to burn or break down the homes of their Apostolics neighbors, confiscate their property, and beat them. Since no one died, they felt totally shocked when officials sent soldiers to give them a taste of what they dished out. The soldiers beat them with rods and the butt of their rifles, and arrested them which astounded the people. Never before had priests been arrested and called to give account of their wrong doing.

Town dwelling Amhara business men who enjoyed being the majority agitated people in the town against the Oromo Administration, but the Oromo lived in the country side. The state fearing war called the leaders of our church and the Orthodox leaders to a meeting at their office. We sent our delegates, Reverend Degu and Reverend Amare. The Orthodox, prepared for bloodshed, refused to come and invited us and the Administration to their church. Knowing their intrigues and pride, and annoyed by the lack of cooperation, the officials made a resolution thanking our delegates and our church for good attitudes and said, "From this day, you can preach freely in this province. If anyone makes a move against you, let us know. We are at your side. We grant you places for graveyards, and to build churches. Be strong."

Officials sent copies of this signed resolution to all Peasant Associations, all other offices, and to whom it may concern. Though the saints rejoiced over the oppression and loss of goods, our delegates had escorts for their safety and the burned houses and lost money got refunded in full. On one reconstruction job, soldiers supervised the men rebuilding what they had destroyed.

Ethiopia has claimed for centuries to have the Ark of the Covenant hidden in a monastery cut out of rock in the hills (no proof). Worship in the Orthodox Church of a miniature ark, representing Moses and the law, has been highly respected for many years. They often have a problem supplying churches with enough of the small, wood-carved replicas. (One district ordered forty-four arks to meet their needs). In the reign of Haile Selasse, they considered these little boxes so sacred one would be fined and imprisoned if he mentioned the arks are made of wood (according to the statutes of law}.

Traditionally, the Oromo worshiped the tree. They reproached the Orthodox saying, "We worship the tree, which is alive; you worship the dry wood that has no life." When they decided to worship Jesus with the Apostolics they would say, "Take away your dry wood and leave us alone."

Some of the Amharas worship a small pot called "Tsewa". They carried it from house to house, supposedly to bring a blessing. One day, on the way to someone's house, the pot slipped, and broke into many pieces. A Moslem saw it and said, "Look, the god of the Amhara is broken!"

We say a god who can be broken is a degraded no-god. The time has come to praise the only true, living God whose name is Jesus.

Saved during Brother Wendell's short time in Ethiopia, Brother Teferi has bravely endured twenty years of persecution--the whole time of his ministry. Arrested and released over and over, his home destroyed and rebuilt several times, he also faced the bitter sorrow of having no place to bury his dead, even on his own land.

In spite of all his hardships, his witness brought many wizards and their patients into the Kingdom who had no hope until he gave them the gospel. Now, at last, he has established a church in Liyu Hamussie, received graveyard rights, and enjoys many blessings. Because of the conversion of many Evangelicals, he recently opened a branch church.

After Brother Tassew laid a good foundation in Gojjam, he came to Debre Berhan in 1992, bought a house and opened a church. This is a place of no religion except for the Orthodox. He knew to live here, he would possibly face death. Just after he began the work, the Amhara went to a Full Gospel prayer meeting and severely beat the people gathered to pray; several died.

God has raised up capable men to assist Tassew who have no fear of death and a mighty revival is sweeping across the land.

In the Gurage tribe, many different dialects are spoken in the Butajira region. Other religions and even missionaries have tried to establish their beliefs in different places among the Gurages, but nothing has lasted among these people except the Orthodox and Islams who cannot lift them out of their sins. Opposition from the people have defeated most efforts.

After a long span of spiritual darkness, some of us went from Sodo to Addis Ababa for school or work. Here God directed us to the Apostolic Church where we found salvation; were baptized in Jesus name, filled with the Holy Ghost, and received a revelation of the mystery of God in Christ. Then, we prayed zealously for the fire of the Gospel to be lit in Butajira.

A word came to us from Ezekiel 2:6,7: *And thou, son of man, be not afraid of them, neither be afraid of their words, though briers and thorns be with thee, and thou dost dwell among scorpions: be not afraid of their words, nor be dismayed at their looks, though they be a rebellious house. And thou shalt speak my words unto them, whether they will hear, or whether they will forbear: for they are most rebellious.*

And chapter 3:11: *And go, get thee to them of the captivity, unto the children of thy people, and speak unto them, and tell them, Thus saith the Lord God; whether they will hear, or whether they will forbear.*

As the message came, we went. We enjoyed our fellowship with each other in our own land and took joy in witnessing. Some received the Word and obeyed the baptism. Since only a few came out of the kingdom of darkness, we had no opposition.

We attended great conferences in Kembattya and Hadya Province and God gave a serious call through Brother Tekle for men to separate themselves for the ministry. The Lord touched my heart, so I took my place standing with the others. The leaders and the congregation prayed for us and my heart filled with zeal. The Lord revealed to some of the brothers what He would do in Butajira, and dreams and visions came to me of my separation for the ministry.

With permission from our Superintendent, I started full time ministry in Addis, but from time to time I returned to Butajira.

In June 1986 I went to a place called Acheber, and they brought a man named Motku Wurgessa, possessed by the devil, to me. Neither holy water nor medicines had helped him, and he lay before me abnormal and unconscious. I first witnessed the oneness of God and the mighty power of Jesus name to those who brought him and they agreed to bow with me in prayer. God's power drove sixty-five demons out of the man and delivered him from his distress. He glorified Jesus.

Astounded by the demonstration of power in Jesus name, the ones who brought the man agreed to listen to the Word explained more fully the next day. I told them how to be completely saved and eight people received the Holy Ghost. I baptized them in Jesus Name.

On my next journey, we had a fellowship at Sibisto that resulted in fifteen baptized in Jesus name and thirteen filled with the Holy Ghost. Another fellowship three weeks later saw sixteen baptized in the name of Jesus and fifteen filled with the Spirit. Three of those saved got deliverance from demon power. One of them, Felekech Mekurria suffered the devil's torment for twelve years. Long separated from her husband, the demons moved her to go to a wizard, bow before him, and pay him tribute. He made her a prisoner in his house, forced her to chew "Khat" daily, and isolated her from her friends and family. She feared to use any utensil used by others and the wizard made her convert to the Islam religion. We prayed in Jesus name and He set her free from every bondage. After baptism in Jesus name she received the Holy Ghost and lives today in peace and rest.

As more people found salvation, the surrounding people began to oppose the preaching of the gospel. At our next fellowship in the home of Brother Dejene Mekuria, the Orthodox priests came at night with a band who had spears, rods, pangas, and rifles. They broke the door down with rods and stones and commenced beating Brother Dejene. Half of the attackers began screaming as if they held a thief and needed more help from the neighbors. Soon a large crowd gathered. When Sister Felekech asked, "Why do you beat my brother?" one of the men threw his panga hoping to cut her in half, but the Lord diverted the big knife. It did not touch her.

As they started to beat the rest of us, differences of opinion between themselves and the bystanders hindered, and finally the majority decided to take us to prison unharmed. The police put the men in one cell and the ladies in another one, both of them very dark. We prayed and sang and praised Jesus all night long. The next day we witnessed to the guards and God touched their hearts to prepare lamps for us. What a wonderful night we had! We studied God's Word together and sang songs in abundance. At 2:00 A.M. with the guards permission, we baptized four people in the name of Jesus.

On the third day, the police asked us to forsake our faith, and if not, we would be punished. All of us replied that we will not forsake our faith and we are ready to accept whatever punishment they would give. Two ladies who had been freed from the devil, but not yet baptized, weakened and agreed to give up their faith. While they discussed it, the demon returned and moved back in where he had lived for fifteen years before we cast him out. One lady started crying and screaming and we began to pray.

The devil answered us and said, "I won't leave her. I've hidden within her all these years and caused her much suffering; the power of Jesus name made me go, but now she has denied His name so I am here to stay."

We kept praying while our opponents watched. Then Jesus gave us victory and Satan had to leave. The people watched the miracle in amazement.

They gave us fines on the fifth day, Twenty Birr for me and ten Birr each for the others and released us the same evening. We were blessed and strengthened by our five days in jail. We went to Brother Dejene's house to continue our night fellowship with joy. We baptized four souls that night and five received the Holy Ghost. From that day the Gospel spread to many places and the number of souls saved increased every day.

We continued our ministry with faith, even though the pattern of being arrested and then released happened repeatedly in different places. God strengthened the newly established churches with miracles, in spite of the persecution that arose against them.

The believers found themselves rejected from the Benevolent Associations and all social activity. They received no help nor consideration in case of accidents, and the people would not even allow their cattle to graze with the saints' cattle. Anyone who greeted them, comforted them in case of sickness or death, or lent them a match or fire received fines varying from 50 to 100 Birr.

Besides having no place to bury their dead, they suffered beatings while their enemies looted and burned their homes. Some were driven out from their families and wandered homeless for the sake of the Gospel, but God made a way of escape for them and they faithfully witnessed, reaching many souls for the Kingdom of God.

Sister Zenebech Mekunia gave us a house for a place of worship at Jolle. We had fellowship there with visiting saints from other churches on Sunday, July 30, 1989 when members of the Orthodox church surrounded us with rods and spears in their hands. They began beating on the windows of our prayer house, hoping to beat us, but God did not allow them. They requested that we accompany them to the local Administration's office and we agreed. When we arrived they had no cell big enough to hold all ninety of us, so they left us outside under guards.

While they are giving false reports to the provincial police, the Party Administration, and the Peasant's Association we continued our fellowship for three days without food or shelter. We sang and prayed and had a full program of great blessings before a committee from every office arrived to question us.

"Why have you gathered such a crowd?"

"We are gathered to pray and worship and teach them the Word of God."

Then they saw Brother Essatu Malle with us, who is a member of the Provincial Peasant Association's court. They knew him well and asked in amazement, "Why do you assemble with these Pentes?"

He answered, "My wife suffered horribly with demon possession for fifteen years, and no one could help her. My oldest son suffered the same affliction from birth and everyone of my family languished in one sickness or another. I am bankrupt because of my family's many problems. Then a man stabbed me in the stomach so deeply my intestines fell on the ground. A sympathetic bystander pushed my intestines back in my stomach and took me to the hospital. As I lay in the hospital without any hope of life I prayed, *God, if you will heal me, I will worship you.*

"God heard my prayer and sent the Apostolics to pray for us and Jesus healed all of us. I will worship Him the rest of my life."

"Enough! the officials yelled, "Stop your preaching!" They sent him out of the office.

They called Sister Zenebech in and asked, "What made you change your religion in your old age?"

"I have not changed, I cling firmly to my religion.'

The official questioned her scornfully, "What do you know?"

"I understand the Word of God says, *He that believeth and is baptized shall be saved.*

"Where is that found?" the official asked in a harsh voice.

She pointed toward me and replied, "Ask the preacher."

The official turned to the Orthodox priests and asked, "Is what the woman said true?"

Sister Zenebech interrupted, "No, No. I don't mean them; I mean our preacher," and pointed again toward me.

Astounded, the questioner asked, "How did they poison her mind?" and sent her out of the office.

They questioned a few more people, then said, "There is no need of further interrogation, because their answers are all the same."

Releasing all the believers except me, they put me in a vehicle to take me to the provincial police office. The Orthodox priests objected, saying, "It is not enough to arrest only him. Take Dejene, and these two women Elfinesh and

Shefaye, too."

Though our Superintendent Tekle came and showed them that our church is legal, the officials could not agree to our release. After eleven days they sentenced us to three months in prison and transferred us to Ziway jail.

From the morning of our entry in jail, we witnessed the word of God to the prisoners. One of them with shackles on his feet hobbled to me and told me the sad story of his life: "I attended a Lutheran mission school until I reached the eleventh grade, then I took a two-year Bible course and worked as a preacher until conflicts between the leaders of the church disillusioned me. I abandoned my faith, forsook God and became a Cadre and went to the battle field answering the call of my country. When I returned from the front line, I received appointment as chairman of the communist party committee in Ziway orphanage school and taught that Christians should be arrested to compel them to deny their faith. I lived a wicked and godless life, and now I am sentenced to death for murdering my wife with a knife. I want to worship God if He will forgive me and have mercy on me."

I gave him the Word of God beginning with true repentance, baptism in Jesus name for the remission of sins, the in-filling of the Holy Ghost, and the Apostle's faith. Though he had not heard these things before and it differed from the teaching he had received, I answered his questions with the Word and he accepted the truth. While I taught him, four others believed and wanted to be baptized, one of them a guard in the prison. The police asked the chief guard for permission and he allowed me to baptize the four men in Lake Ziway, but not the man with the death sentence.

God's glory on my life made the soldiers and the

chairman of the prison respect and love me, so that we avoided many of the problems that prisoners usually have. The chairman said, "Four days before you came, a man I did not know came to me as I sat alone in my office and told me,'Messengers of God will come to this jail. Take care of them.' I do not understand if perhaps the man is an angel, but I am at your service."

We had many discussions on the scriptures and became well acquainted. He testified to the commanders of the prison, "Since these men of God came to this jail, everything is peaceful. Before they came we had many sick prisoners and deaths often, now everyone recovers and none has died."

I went to him one day with a request, "The man who is sentenced to death has requested me to baptize him. I will be grateful if you can help us find a way."

He answered, "I'm glad he wants to obey the Lord, and I'll do my best to help him. I'll let you know as soon as possible."

He called me two days later and said, "I found the answer--here in the jail."

Surprised and happy, I asked, "Where?"

He told me about a partly buried water tank unused at the moment. I rejoiced that God had prepared this for a needy soul inside the prison compound. The Chairman came to the prison the next morning at four o'clock, sent soldiers to bring me and the condemned man and ordered other soldiers to fill the tank with water. By a wondrous miracle, I baptized a man waiting to die in the name of Jesus.

We had applied to different officials for our release explaining we had been imprisoned unlawfully. They finally released us on the fifty-fifth day. Brother Yohannes

Estifanos, the condemned man wanted to sing one song for us before we left, so we went to his cell. As he sang about the remission of his sin weeping the Spirit of the Lord fell on him and he glorified God with other tongues, rolling on the ground. We praised our God with tears because of His great goodness.

After a few days I went back to the prison and baptized eighteen more souls in Jesus name with the aid of the prison Chairman and the chief guards. We rejoiced that our time spent in jail gave us twenty-three souls.

Brother Yohannes asked reconsideration of his case and got transferred to Addis Ababa jail where he witnessed faithfully sending a stream of seekers, whose trials ended, to us for baptism.

I applied to the regional Attorney's office and received permission to preach the Gospel freely and asked that the cases of our brethren who suffered persecution should be solved lawfully. As a result, the executives of twelve localities were called to the head office and commanded not to give us any more problems. This gave us liberty to worship freely.

Those who had opposed us died with the plague and the rest went to the wizards and to wise elders for advice and both of them gave the same answer; "Stop opposing these people because they worship one God. You can't eliminate them by opposition, and if you continue, God will bring more plagues on this place."

Some hardened their hearts, because God wanted to teach a lesson on what happens to people who oppose His work. Many more prominent ones died with the plague and the others terrified said, "We must be careful not to do anything against these Pentes, all those who came against them have perished and besides, no hardship or suffering will make them deny their faith."

In some places they asked the Apostolics to return to the Benevolent Association saying, "We put you out trying to change you. Now, we understand no matter what happens, you will hold fast to your religion, so we want you to come back and let your cattle graze with ours."

In other places they stopped attacking us face to face, but they devised more subtle ways to hinder us saying, "If you do not come back to your old church, we will send you to the front lines of the battle field, and you will not return."

Some of our men went to the battle front and returned declaring firmly, "Jesus Christ saves!"

Today, with our rights protected by the constitution, we have our own graveyard and God has performed so many miracles the families of our persecutors have found true salvation. We have sixteen churches in Butajira and when the scattered saints are gathered together, it will be twenty. Ten denominational preachers now preach the true Gospel.

Kembatta and Hadiya

When friends and families of Erkenesh and Tekle chased them away because of the gospel, Mekonnen Ludamo, the cousin of Erkenesh, shared their problems and their faith. He is now the presbyter of this section. He has experienced bitter hatred from enemies of the gospel and God's power to deliver when evil men encircled his house many times determined to kill him.

During the reign of the Derg, they confiscated Mekonnen's land for collective farming and forced him to be a member causing him multiple hardships. A few days before the fall of the Derg, men came to destroy his church. Held by the Spirit of God, he answered boldly, "Jesus Christ knows who will be destroyed." Confused, they left without lifting a hand.

After the fall of the Derg, the people rose up and dismantled the big houses, offices and stores built by forced labor, and carried all the materials away not leaving even a stick behind. Immediately the local chairman accused Mekennon saying, "Mekennon has destroyed these houses because he told us he knew what would be destroyed." The administrator knowing the facts refused to accept the case, leaving his accusers in shame.

Brother Mekonnen applied for permission to build a church on that land, but his relatives planned to kill him claiming, "The land belonged to our great grandfather and we are his heirs." The Lord took his opponents and the land was given to the Apostolic church of Ethiopia. In the place where communist youth once gathered in large halls to denounce Christianity, a magnificent church stands to the glory of Jesus Christ.

God did miracles even under the communist regime. They gave us a large tract of land in 1987 where we built a church and had much acreage for crops and pasture

Brother Elias who trained in the Bible school in Nairobi, Kenya came to Hossana. With his meek spirit and persuasive witness, he won Brother Yosef and many others to the Lord. He served the district as secretary for a long time and now provides capable leadership in the Evangelistic ministry.

In repeated conferences in Watto, we have successfully converted many nominal preachers to the truth. In 1987 the SIM prepared their conference near to ours in order to prevent their people attending our services. As our meeting progressed in power, we sang in the Spirit and our singing could be heard more than a mile. Under the sound of that anointed singing the Holy Ghost fell on the honest-hearted attending the SIM conference and they fell on their knees weeping and speaking in other tongues.

Their leaders became very angry. The thing they despised and had forbidden fell upon their people in front of them. They grabbed rods and began beating the people on the head bringing considerable confusion. Half of the people ran out and came to our conference where we worshiped in joy and unity.

The leaders went to the Administrator asking them to arrest all the people who say, "The Holy Ghost has fallen on me." The Administrator replied, "I have nothing to do with religion. Go solve your problems according to your books."

In a very short time, the Lord gave us one hundred seventy-five churches in that area; we have 121,500 members baptized in Jesus name and filled with the Holy Ghost in our section.

In December 1987 we witnessed the mighty power of God in the dedication of Brother Arkeno's church which can accommodate two thousand people. We did not know the enemies of the church planned to have us arrested en masse but their plans failed because of the enormous crowd and their armed helpers who failed to materialize.

We went free, but they arrested Brother Arkeno as a criminal the next day. Armed men threw him in a dark cell where insects tormented him and horrible odors suffocated him for seventeen days. Then the secretary of the communist party office and the district Administrator sentenced him to three months in prison, but the judge bravely released him with surety. We are sure this happened because the church prayed for him continuously. The Derg fell soon after this and the comrades fled and ended their persecution of Brother Arkeno.

We only realized how God defended us when we learned that in a place not too far from us Orthodox priests hanged an Evangelical preacher. They exhumed the body and tried to burn it, and finally gave the remains to the dogs. The police found dogs fighting over it, took pictures for evidence, and reburied the pitiful remains.

The zealous youth of our division out gave the young people of all other sections. Our Fathers group and the Ladies Auxiliary lagged behind until they realized the truth of an Ethiopian proverb: *If threads cooperate they can tie a lion.* Now, everyone feels the responsibility of supporting the spread of the Gospel message throughout Ethiopia.

The Conference at Wa Gebeta

Wa Gebeta means God's dish in Hadiya. It is a fertile plain surrounded by mountains. We planned our conference for December 24, 1992, even though this is the time of rain. We began the services in faith. The other denominational leaders forgot the power of God and hired a famous wizard at a high price to bring rain and thunder to hinder us. He went to the mountain for three days stretching his arms like Balaam alternately toward our assembly and toward heaven. The rain poured down on him where he stood but when it came toward the place of our conference the wind dispersed it to return to the wizard.

We completed our planned three-day conference with tremendous blessings, without rain. Many followers of the

Christians in name only came to us when they saw the farce. They opened their homes to the Apostolics with great respect; no one spent the night outside. Many souls sought baptism in Jesus name and declared they saw the hand of God move as never before.

After observing the blessing one nominal pastor returned to his saints and said, "I will never be the same again. A special secret of heaven has been revealed to me, and I cannot be your pastor as I have been in the old spirit. I stand before you to say goodbye..."

His congregation interrupted him by standing and saying in unison, "Share with us the secret of heaven which is revealed to you. We want to know. If something is wrong, we apologize, but do not leave us. Teach us what you have learned."

Today that congregation has obeyed the truth and listens to the true Gospel in every service. Missionaries brought wheat to one church to buy their loyalty. The people answered, "We will take the wheat from you and the Gospel from the Apostolics." Since they could not take it back, the missionaries gave them the wheat and the next day we baptized all of them in the name of Jesus and those not filled received the Holy Ghost. In those months we baptized over ten thousand people.

In Shensheto Zebego, a famous wizard died; apparently Satan strangled him. As his followers gathered to bury him, the demons that had lived in him attacked them. They felt unseen rods beating them with unseen hands and they collided with each other; their heads knocked against each other's heads by an unseen force. They could neither stand nor sit and did not know how to get deliverance from this evil power, but one of them finally suggested, "Let us go to the Apostolics." When we prayed they found deliverance and much more.

Students who graduated from Niarobi Bible School

Church at Negele Borna near Somali border

269 preachers ordained in 1993

Building!

CHAPTER TWENTY-ONE

AND THE WORK PROSPERED

By Tekle

Addis Ababa is a key city of many regions and here the Lord gives us opportunities to touch many different people with the Gospel. We reached out and first opened four branch works and later six more. At this time we have thirteen branch works, often baptizing thirty or more each week. Brother Ayele Lakew ably pastors the original Gofa church and is the leader of the Addis Ababa section with twelve fine men working under him.

For a long time we have met with the preachers regularly twice a week to teach and encourage them. No one has interrupted or hindered this work. Government regulations demanded that all religions get permission before planning a meeting. We knew if we asked permission, the answer would be *no*, so we asked the Lord and continued with our meetings that are wonderfully blessed. With the proclamation of democracy we hastened to rent houses in every village where we can gather the people together. Now, we sing and pray and preach and worship freely in the Holy

Ghost, and the Lord gives the increase.

Our General Conference increased to more than ten thousand people, but the rain made things difficult. Since the saints could not find a dry place to sleep, we felt compelled to plan a 14,531 square foot building with a large balcony. When I told the people about the need, I estimated its cost at three million Birr; we only had a hundred thousand Birr. But, I insisted, "Let us rise up and build by faith. The Lord will accomplish the work if we are willing."

An amazing dedication to work seized the people and both old and young grabbed hoes and began digging the foundation with vigor. From digging the ground to raising the columns, the builders had no rest for the people pressed into their hands all the needed materials. The work went speedily and our hearts rejoiced to see the building grow larger each day. Within four months we completed the great house for God, lacking only rafters and the sheet iron roof.

Just as in Bible times, God has moved on the hearts of the people to give, not only their land but also their money. Some gave a hundred thousand Birr, some fifty thousand and many ten thousand. Many of those gifts represented considerable sacrifice. Colonel Fidda willingly gave a part of his land for a branch church.

Furious about the construction of the enormous building, other religious leaders tried to find someone to kill me. A man named Abate thought he would please God by eliminating me so he paid Assab 35 Birr for a sword and came to church with a pocket full of rocks and the sword concealed in his clothing. He planned to throw a stone at my head and when I fell, he would quickly put his sword in my stomach and escape through a window. Just as he thought to carry out his plan, he saw the angel of the Lord standing behind me with a glittering sword held aloft in his hand. He fled in terror.

As Abate brooded over his failure, he finally worked up his courage to try again. This time the same angel threatened him with his magnificent sword and he hastily threw the stones out the window, crawled under a bench trembling, and whimpered over and over, "Forgive me." After a time he confessed his evil plans and requested that every preacher present pray for him; he then asked to be baptized in the name of Jesus. The people rejoiced mightily over God's unfailing protection, even when no one knew danger had come to church.

Brother Abate has untiringly used his welding skills on windows, doors, roofing and wherever needed in the construction of the conference center, saving us considerable costs.

A man named Shume came to church with a heart full of hatred determined to kill me. The anointed preaching of the Word crushed his heart and revealed Truth to him. He repented with many tears, confessing his intentions before the people. Today in Hagere Mariam he preaches the Gospel he once hated.

We erected a tent inside the walls of the building to protect the crowd from rain for our 1992 Conference. Our guests from America assembled with us: Brother Cleveland Becton, General Secretary of the United Pentecostal Church International; Brother Harry Scism, Foreign Missions director; Brother J.P. Hughes, Regional Field Supervisor for Africa; with their wives and others.

Rain fell freely the previous night filling the canvas top above our heads and the height did not allow workers to tip the water out before the day service began. Brother

Becton brought a wonderful message with many prophesies and then asked for the Amharic word meaning water. We told him *wuha*. He explained as a natural cloud carries the water and pours it upon the earth so our omnipresent God can pour the Holy Spirit upon us. He cried out, "Wuha! Wuha!" and without wind or a human hand touching it, the canvas overhead spilled it's contents on the worshipers. The Holy Ghost moved on them mightily; they spoke in other tongues as trees bent by the wind. Those on whom the water fell regarded it as extraordinary grace and rejoiced in being soaked! This story is told repeatedly all over the land as a wonderful demonstration of God's great power.

Journalists from the media recorded the happening and wanted to broadcast it on the news. The zealot enemies of the church tried to block them. The journalists replied, *If we don't transmit the true stories about this church, whose should we tell? The other churches are cold and lifeless.*

In this glorious day of opportunity, God has anointed many workers to proclaim the true Gospel in Addis. And Satan has raised up many false prophets to mislead the people, but their efforts can be defeated by prayer and fasting.

A group of hungry hearted people met together in Akaki and fasted and prayed for eight months, asking the Lord to reveal His truth to them--and He did. They thought no one but them had this revelation, since it came from heaven and no man had taught them. One of our brothers visited them and heard a taped song at their house that made him curious.

He asked, "What is your belief?"

"We believe that Jesus Christ is Lord of all, He is Jehovah manifested in flesh."

Excitedly, the brother replied, "That is the belief of my church, the Apostolic church of Ethiopia! Here, let me give you some tracts and booklets of the church."

Though they had not heard of the church before, a large number of them came to Addis in 1992 for baptism in the name of Jesus. They returned home to teach the truth to people rejected by the Orthodox Church because they read the Bible. No doubt, we will soon build a big church in Akaki, for many are following the Lord, though they assemble in houses now.

How beautiful upon the mountains are the feet of him that bringeth good tidings; that publisheth peace; that bringeth tidings of good, that publisheth salvation; that saith unto Zion, thy God reigneth (Isaiah 52:7).

Nona Freeman explains "At the Louisiana camp Meeting in 1991, Billy Cole came to me, with a question, `Tekle has promised me a crowd of fifty thousand if I come to Ethiopia to preach. Can he do it?'"

I answered, "If Tekle promises you fifty thousand, he will not only provide that big an audience, but probably two or three times more. His word is good."

In March of 1992, Billy and a group of preachers and friends went, not knowing what to expect, but he felt led to believe God for the unheard of: ten thousand filled with the Holy Ghost at one time. The gruelling trip to Wara tested the endurance of those who went, flat tires, engine problems, misunderstandings, name it, they had it.

On the Saturday, they gave several hours of Bible teaching to prepare people whose hunger for God moved them to come in spite of circumstances. They walked long distances, rode cars and trucks (not roadworthy) loaded beyond reason, and ramshackle buses that groaned under the weight of people crammed inside and clinging outside like flies. After a few short messages, testimonies, and songs, and a confusing division of the haves and have nots, they came to the point Billy felt God's time had come and he stretched out his hand toward the have nots and cried with authority, "Receive ye the Holy Ghost!" Instantly thousands of voices burst out speaking in other tongues as the Holy Ghost gave the utterance in fulfillment of the Word *And it shall come to pass in the last days saith God, I will pour out of my Spirit upon all flesh...*(Acts 2:17).

They made a conservative estimate of twenty thousand filled with the Spirit. When we attended the preachers conference and dedication of the E.L. Freeman conference center in February, 1993, we found the believers fasting and praying for a repeat of the 1992 meetings the following month. Brother Tekle told us that as the people filled with the Spirit sought the nearest church for baptism in the name of Jesus, pastors accumulated records of over forty thousand who received the Pentecostal experience that phenomenal Sunday. (I have never known anyone to keep records as meticulously as the Apostolics of Ethiopia.)

Tekle continues. Not long after the 1992 crusade in Wara about thirty thugs came with a truck and attacked our two guards whom they beat with iron bars and stabbed. Leaving them for dead they broke in our front door. Erkenesh tried to hide under a small table, but I felt no fear and threw my shoes at these men armed with guns, momentarily distracting their attention. I heard some of them breaking in the back door and ran there. As they pushed the door open I slammed it shut knocking them down. Frightened by an angel with a flaming sword in his hand they ran to the front of the house and I slipped out. By the power of Jesus I climbed over the ten foot high wall with broken glass and barbed wire at the top without injury and hurried to a friend's house to call the police.

Meanwhile the thieves wasted time trying to find me and managed to steal only two video decks before the police came. The police took some of the vandals into custody; others escaped. One man grabbed the sack of Sunday School offering and tried to escape over the back fence. He made it with injuries that left a trail of blood, but had to drop the sack of money inside where we retrieved it. We took the guards to the hospital for stitches and prayed for them and the Lord healed them completely. They told us the men came to kill our whole family, take everything of value they could find, and destroy the church building. Again, the name of Jesus saved us from the merciless sword of the enemy.

Work on the Conference Center progressed. While lifting one of the one-ton steel beams to hold the roof, those on the ends with ropes to guide it misunderstood instructions. Instead of holding steady, they turned loose. The beam fell on me and though it cruelly crushed my leg, I thanked God for sparing my life. I disobeyed doctor's instructions to stay off my leg and hobbled on crutches to supervise completion of the task. This trial of pain lasted over a year before the Great Physcian touched me and made me whole.

March, 1993 found Billy Cole with another team of helpers, prayer warriors, and notable visitors on their way to Wara in Sidamo for the second miracle crusade. Brother Harry Scism, Director of Foreign Missions; Brother Kenneth Haney, an editor, Superintendent of Christian Life College, and pastor of an unusual mission-minded church made the never-easy journey to revival, along with Bobbye Wendell, widow of Kenneth Wendell. These folks who pioneered the opening of Ethiopia to the Gospel deserve the highest commendation.

Reading and hearing the reports from the privileged witnesses, one feels a distinct inadequacy in the power of words to describe the indescribable. Which one of us with our sedate, well-ordered life in the Western world can picture twenty-eight people leaping and crawling over obstacles to lay prone sobbing and praising God in front of the platform and declare, "I am one of those raised from the dead!"

How can we understand the spiritual hunger of people standing for six hours of Bible teaching? With our comfort-oriented culture, can we believe the massive crowds, one hundred fifty thousand and upwards standing attentively for all the services? *I wonder how many of those who made any one of these three trips grasped the significance of the sacrificial, non-covetous, truly humble ministry of Ethiopia?*

The wonder works of blind eyes opened, all manner of diseases and infirmities healed pale in the light of the forty thousand souls Billy Cole claimed and saw filled with the Holy Ghost as a mighty torrent of the Spirit poured down from heaven to overflow hungry hearts. A glorious postscript comes from examining records of those seeking baptism later--more than sixty thousand claim God filled them with His power that day in one service. The greatest record in the history of the church!

In the third crusade March 1994, Billy Cole said with humility, "This time, I made no claims, we simply went trusting our Omnipotent Savior to work His divine will in every life." We are confident that along with the known miracles of healing and deliverance, many others will only be confirmed when the Books are opened and the whole story is revealed. Varying estimates of the number filled with the Holy Ghost start at twenty thousand and go up. Those refilled increases the number considerably. Final figures of *how many* are not the essence of this tremendous happening. The point is: Jesus Christ is ready to fulfil His Word and pour out His Spirit all over the world!

The wizards, hired by the denominational leaders to prevent Apostolic conferences in Wara, killed eithty-one bulls in nine different sessions and conceded that nothing would stop the blessing of these conferences and left the area. Their hinderance gone allowed the Spirit to pour out freely on hungry souls. (Full story in Chapter Nine.) This is a witness the devil cannot hinder the latter day outpouring here or anywhere else in the world.

Knowing their faithfulness under suffering, I am not surprised the Book of Acts continues in Ethiopia.

I long for the glory to fall on all the rest of this sin-wracked globe!

Choir in roofless building

Visitors, including Bectons, in roofless
Conference Center

Congregation blessed by Wahu during
Brother Becton's message

CHAPTER TWENTY-TWO

FLASH!

Flash! A phone call from Tekle gave us thrilling reports of recent miracles. In the Duguna area of Wollayta, a sweeping revival broke out that dismayed the SIM who are strong in that part of the country. They launched fierce persecution against the Apostolic church.

Justifying their actions they met to fast and pray. A strange cat landed on the rafters of their church and told them in their own language: *Go to the Apostolic church.* It repeated the sentence over and over. They tried to kill the cat, but it ran away. They said, "This is ridiculous; we will not tell anyone that a cat spoke to us."

The cat went to a house with the same message, and the embarrassed householders ran it off their property. It came to the home of an elderly lady who listened in amazement. "How interesting! This cat is talking to me in my own language."

She then she called her neighbors to hear the cat's message. These witnesses made it impossible to deny the phenomena. Those who heard the cat hunted the Apostolic church, though they had never heard of it before.

The next day an angel struck the roof of the SIM church like lightning; it split open and burst into flames. People fell right and left crawling to escape the fire. The angel went out the front gate and a bottomless hole appeared between the church building and the front gate. The fear of God sent many people hurrying to the Apostolic church to seek salvation.

Nomad moslems live in a vast area appointed them by the government. Their lifestyle and stiff distrust of strangers have made it almost impossible to reach them with the gospel. An angel came to one of them and said, "Go to Valea in Jemjem.

When the Lord spoke to Hiele Gamede to take strange nomads the Word of God, he knew they could easily kill him. He fasted and prayed earnestly before attempting to obey. He walked into a group of them with his Bible in his hand and began to read to them chapter after chapter.

The Nomads did not hinder him. the Lord made them think *this man is one of us*. But when he began to speak, they started yelling and screaming and rolling on the ground. Gamede spent several busy moments rebuking the devil who possessed everyone of them.

When the last person got deliverance, the Holy Ghost fell, and, not knowing what was happening to them, eighty-six ex-Moslems received the baptism of the Holy Ghost.

This started an outstanding revival among the Moslems that continues to spread across the countryside.

The daughter of a well-known Moslem leader suffered horrible attacks from Satan. Her father observed the power manifested by the Apostolics and said, "I do not want to convert to this new religion, but I will give them my daughter and perhaps they can help her. "

With her father present, Brother Gamede prayed for the daughter and she received instant healing and the in-filling of the Holy Ghost. Her father is now a troubled man, trying to avoid surrender to Jesus.

In Fiche, the sub-district of Shonkalie, a huge python full of demons lived in a grove and ruled by speaking to the people in the Oromo language. His witch doctor side-kick collected protection money from the terrified populace. No matter how much they paid, it seemed they could not protect their children; frequently the python swallowed one of them.

Yadeti, a man possessed of Satan for twenty years lived in this area. One day his cattle went crazy. For a year they bellowed and carried on strangely. Seeking help, he found a denominational minister who helped him overcome his problems, and, without understanding the words, quoted Acts 2:38 to him. Then the preacher wanted to baptize him in the titles, but Yadeti left for Addis Ababa determined to find someone to baptize him in the name of Jesus.

One of the brothers witnessed to him and brought him to the church where he rejoiced to go down in the water according to Acts 2:28. After the Lord mightily filled him with the Holy Ghost, he determined to return home to preach the Apostolic message to his people bound by the worship of the python.

Yadeti faced defiant opposition and even after many struggles, only twenty people believed the message. then God gave him a scripture: Isaiah 57:13,14: *...but he that putteth his trust in me shall possess the land, and shall inherit my holy mountain; And shall say, Cast ye up, cast ye up,* *prepare the way, take up the stumbling block out of the way of my people.*

As the python opposed him personally, he rebuked him in Jesus name, backed by the Word of God. A big wind came; the snake rose up in the air screaming, "The other churches have not bothered me, but your strange gospel takes away my power. I am leaving."

The preacher and his helpers began cutting down the grove and the witch doctor yelled, "I will not help you anymore." They paid no attention, having found a better way.

In desperation the witch doctor sent his servant with a gun and much ammunition. He attempted to shoot Brother Yadeti and one of his helpers in the back, but an angel covered them. The bullets fell harmlessly to the ground.

The saints gathered up the bullets and showed them to the Commissioner, telling him the story. He sent the police to arrest the would-be murderer who fled. They found him and put him in prison. The Commissioner announced to the whole region: "The Apostolic church is free to worship where ever they will, and no one must hinder them. They have brought great benefit to our region."

The miracles began with a forty year old insane woman who, for twenty years, had roamed the woods naked and ate grass. An angel led her to the church and Jesus delivered her. Now it is a joy to watch her dance before the Lord as she lives a useful life with a mind made normal and dedicated to God.

An incredible number of blind, lame, and diseased people have been healed; the demon-possessed are free, and many have risen from the dead as revival sweeps across the land like fire leaping through dead grass.

Brother J.P. Hughes RFS for Africa
preaching dedication of Conference Center

Freemans, Brother Urshan, and Tekle in
front of Conference Center

Thirteen thousand ministers and workers
attend dedication

Sister Scism cuts welcome cake

Brother Urshan with Tekle at dedication

Youth Choir

Brother Kilgore with Tekle at conference

Kilgores with Tekle and Erkenesh

Billy Cole arriving at Wara

Part of the crowd

Billy Cole and Missionary Bruce Howell at
Wara Crusade

Brother Kenneth Haney preaching at
crusade

Offering

Ready to go!

194

Worshiping!

Sidamo presbyters

195

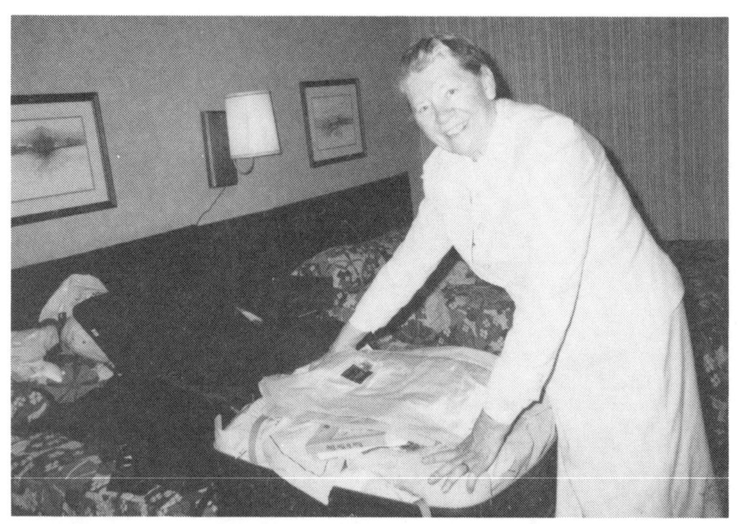

Nona helping Tekle pack to return home
from USA

Erkenesh, Thetus Tenney, and Nona
Freeman with Ethiopian ladies

196

CHAPTER TWENTY-THREE

ERKENESH PROMOTED

By Nona Freeman

SEPTEMBER 17, Saturday, Stockton, CA, Conference:
"Tekle! So happy to see you. How is my dear friend Erkenesh?"

"God has healed her of paralysis from the stroke she had. She can walk again and use her hand. We will soon be able to travel as we did before."

SEPTEMBER 22, Thursday:
Message to Tekle from his family: "Come home as quickly as possible. Erkenesh is dying."

SEPTEMBER 24, Saturday:
Tekle arrived at his home in Addis Ababa to learn Erkenesh died on Thursday. When her family entered her room that morning, she appeared to be sleeping peacefully with closed mouth and eyes, but they could not waken her. The doctor (a relative) came and pronounced her dead. Later

they took her to the hospital where other doctors pronounced her dead, but her body remained fresh and soft without rigor mortis and with no sign of deterioration until they laid her away.

SEPTEMBER 25, Sunday:

Five thousand people gathered in the conference center in Addis Ababa to bid farewell to the beloved mother of revival in Ethiopia. The suddenness of her home-going prevented thousands more from attending.

SEPTEMBER 26, Monday:

Tekle boarded the plane to return to the USA to speak at the General Conference of the United Pentecostal Church International held in Milwaukee, Wisconsin.

OCTOBER 2, Sunday:

One of three speakers in a tremendous mission service, Tekle inspired his listeners with a positive report of miracles and revival in his land based on Bible obedience.

That night, after a song by the Indiana Bible college, a wave of exuberant worship swept over the thousands in attendance. Tekle became the focal point as he danced and rejoiced across the large platform. Sometimes kneeling with his face to the floor, sometimes leaping, he continued unabated for over an hour. Realizing he had buried his wife of twenty-five years only a week before, the audience responded with an unprecedented depth of adoration to the King of Kings.

Miracles began happening all over the huge auditorium. A deaf man's ears opened. A woman in a wheel chair for three years stood and walked upon the platform to give her testimony. Many received the Holy Ghost. Healing and restoration poured across the crowd like a benevolent river in flood. Only heaven's recording angel knows the extent of the miraculous deliverances in this remarkable service.

Feeling extreme heaviness of Spirit two years ago, Tekle fasted and prayed continually for seven days without sleep. Just as his time of seeking God ended, Erkenesh had a stroke and died, remaining lifeless for thirty minutes until he called her back in the name of Jesus. She returned saying, "Not yet; not yet."

She told him of the steps she made on her journey to heaven. At the first step an angel asked her, "What is the greatest commandment?"

"There is one God and I must love Him with all my heart, soul, and mind."

The angel said, "Proceed to the second step."

At the second step the question came, "What is the second commandment?"

"I must love my neighbor as myself."

"Proceed to the third step."

Then another angel intervened, "Go back; it is not yet time."

Seven months later with malaria and another stroke she died again and lay lifeless for forty-five minutes until Tekle's prayers brought her back. She told him by sign language then, "I want to go."

Before our visit in '93, I phoned her son Abraham for a report on her condition. He answered, "She recognizes no one, cannot speak, and her right arm and leg is paralyzed." Brother Freeman and I went to Brother Tom Barnes asking prayer for dear, prayer warrior Erkenesh. After prayer, he told us, "Lay hands on her and pray; she will recognize you and talk to you, but the third problem will only be healed later." It happened just as he said.

When her death brought Tekle home from America in '94, feeling his whole world had collapsed, he fell across his wife's body and prayed, "Lord, I cannot make it without her." But before he could continue, Jesus answered, *Do not ask me to send her back. I wanted to take her two years ago, but you are holding her back. It is time for her to rest; let her go.* Only heaven knows the anguish this revelation brought, but God's son bowed again to the will of God.

Later the Lord brought vivid scenes to his mind showing her powerful testimonies and how thoroughly Erkenesh had prepared for her going. She handed her leadership over to hand picked, capable ladies in every area of the land. She organized chains of fasting and prayer, once a week all-night prayer meetings, arranged financial support for home missionaries, and a method of raising money to support missionaries in foreign lands.

God often used Erkenesh in diversities of spiritual gifts. She had the word of knowledge and wisdom, excellent discernment, and blessed the church with her gift of prophecy. She had amazing linguistic talent, able to read and write and speak in nine different languages which enabled her to minister to people of many races. She immersed herself in each new language she encountered with a fierce determination to conquer it. Her value in establishing the church in Ethiopia cannot be measured in words. Never have I seen a more gracious and thoughtful hostess. She entertained every visitor with acute awareness, "This guest could be an angel in disguise."

But, above all these things, Erkenesh excelled in prayer. She majored in prayer. With small children and a continuous stream of guests, she never failed to spend at least three hours a day seeking the Lord. Though she loved her children devotedly, I remember her joy when her youngest child started to school, "Oh, now I can pray longer without interruptions."

Tekle said Erkenesh seldom slept more than two hours a night. She spent most nights on her knees. She literally wore out her body in deep intercession. When we travelled together in America in 1986 for six weeks sleeping in motels, I would lift her from her knees at two or three o'clock in the morning with, "Dear, you must get some rest; we are facing another busy day." She rejoiced when we had separate rooms and I couldn't bother her.

Erkenesh's candle of life burned brilliantly with no consideration for comfort or desire for earthly goods, but, oh, what a harvest of souls she laid at the Master's feet!

Called away at age forty-seven she left her husband Tekle, fifty-seven.

Daughter Mehret, twenty-three, mother of her three grandchildren.

Son Josias, twenty-one.

Son Abraham, nineteen.

Daughter Jerusalem, seventeen.

Son Joshua, fifteen.

And thousands upon thousands of spiritual children.

How beautiful resurrection day will be!